Michael Williams

Bossiney Books

First published in 1982
by Bossiney Books
St. Teath, Bodmin, Cornwall
Designed, typeset and printed in Great Britain by
Penwell Ltd, Parkwood, Callington
Cornwall

ISBN 0 906456 65 7

PLATE ACKNOWLEDGMENTS

Front Cover by Ray Bishop
Back Cover by Richard Isbell
Pages 5, 7, 8 David Golby
Pages 31, 47, 49, 53, 55, 66, 69, 71, 74 Ray Bishop
Pages 77, 78, 81 Alice Lennox-Boyd
Pages 13, 59, 73 Mike Frost
Page 23 Southgate Studio
Page 15 The Broadway family album
Page 90 Paul Honeywill
Page 87 George Ellis
Page 92 David Clarke
All other photographs by Richard Isbell

About the Author—and the Book

A Cornishman, Michael Williams started full time publishing in 1975. With his wife Sonia, he runs Bossiney Books from a cottage and converted barn in North Cornwall — they are literally Cornish cottage publishers, specializing in Westcountry subjects by Westcountry authors.

For ten years they ran the Bossiney House Hotel, just outside Tintagel — hence the name Bossiney Books. Then in 1975 they left the hotel business and moved to St Teath. This is their 79th title.

Here in **Superstition and Folklore**, Michael Williams says: '. . . superstition curiously is not on its deathbed. Almost as if to contradict the disappearance of old expressions and little rituals, there is in some quarters, a return to superstition.'

Romany reflections, old country customs, interviews with superstitious people, folklore from both Devon and Cornwall, omens, and coincidences are all featured in this, his 11th book for Bossiney.

'Superstition may not be quite as old as the hills, but its roots go back to the early first light of Man's story . . . remnants of old religions and beliefs — and magical ritual.'

SUPERSTITION and FOLKLORE

In 1981 my wife Sonia heard two bells simultaneously: someone ringing the door bell to our cottage and the phone starting to ring.

'That's a sign of death,' she said, later. It was something I'd never heard before—either the superstition or two bells sounding at the same moment. Almost as if to confirm the omen, a large Cornish sea painting, in our dining room, crashed to the floor that weekend. Within a week Sonia had news that her aunt had died. Though aged and in a nursing home there had been no warning of her sudden demise.

Superstition may not be quite as old as the hills but its roots go back to the early first light of Man's story, and that's not surprising when you study the very word 'superstition' because it comes from the old Latin *superstites,* meaning survivors. The plain fact is many of our superstitions are just that: survivors from the long ago. The majority of them are the remnants of old religions and beliefs—and magical ritual.

Luck is an essential ingredient in many lives. Luck is a mysterious element—like a pot of gold at the end of a rainbow. Probably as many as nine people out of ten look for luck—and hope for it.

There is a German saying which goes: 'Luck follows the hopeful, ill luck the fearful.' And that's pretty logical when you think of Jung, the famous Swiss psychologist, who evolved the theory called 'Synchronicity' in which he put forward the idea that the psychological condition of man or woman *attracts* events to him or her. This, of course, ties in with that ancient Romany expression: 'Think lucky and you'll be lucky'.

'I love old churches and their yards: but I have always trod carefully . . . avoiding stepping on a grave.' ▶

I have to admit that a strong current of superstition has always run through my life. Some of it conscious—and some of it somehow there yet not crystal-clear. Take, for instance, churchyards. I love old churches and their yards; but always I have trod carefully—even as a boy—deliberately avoiding stepping on a grave. Only years later did I discover Coleridge's words:

To see a man tread over graves,
I hold it no good mark;
'Tis wicked in the sun and moon,
And bad luck in the dark!

Something locked in memory or instinct had always warned me.

Each generation considers itself wiser than its predecessor, and yet some things continue to baffle, to elude explanation.

Some of the contents of this book may, at first glance, appear slightly sinister but I like to think this is due to their 'otherworldliness'. In researching into the Supernatural, I am constantly reminded of the healer who told me 'These things are not Supernatural . . . they're Supernormal!' As far as the Westcountry is concerned, I am sure that there is more magical or spiritual quality here than in most places.

The discovery of origin in superstition—where and when possible—can be intriguing. It's unlucky, for example, to be the third cigarette lit from the same match. This theory was developed in the Boer War when soldiers would cluster for a cigarette, and the enemy sniper would often be able to 'pick off' the third soldier: the first light giving away their position, and the second light giving the sniper a chance to take aim. Sonia, once a smoker, told me that though she had never heard of the smoking superstition, she never lit a third cigarette from a lighter without clicking the lighter off and back on after the second cigarette had been lit. Something somewhere in her memory *made* her click the lighter after that second cigarette.

Twenty years ago, I should have thought seriously about the wisdom of either writing or publishing this book. Though cynical Doubting Thomases, like the poor, will always be among us, the

**'To see a man tread over graves,
I hold it no good mark.' Coleridge ▶**

'Superstition may not be quite as old as the hills, but its roots go back to the early first light of Man's story . . . there is more magical or spiritual quality here in the Westcountry than in most places.'

last decade has seen a radical and more tolerant attitude come into being. A policeman can now sight a puma or a phantom black dog and not lose his uniform. Academics can write about fork-bending or clairvoyancy and not be stripped of their degrees. But it must have been a brave or foolish Editor of *The Redruth Independent* who published a story in 1886 about snails that fell out of an August sky near Redruth.

It has been my privilege and pleasure to interview more than two hundred people, claiming unusual experiences, happenings that have ranged from sightings of ghosts to premonitions, poltergeists to palmistry. Supernatural is, in fact, a large umbrella, covering many facets. Moreover seeing is not always believing. I once talked to a lady, who owned a haunted house in Cornwall, and though she had *heard* inexplicable knockings on doors and had seen those same doors open and shut without human aid, she still refused to believe her house was haunted and dismissed the possibility of Supernatural happenings. But she was happily in a tiny minority.

Happily, too, I encountered very few interviewees who failed to convince me. In earlier books, like *Supernatural in Cornwall* and *Occult in the West*, I made facts my objective. Where and when inconsistency or inaccuracy occurred, events never went beyond my notebook.

Peter Underwood, in his *Dictionary of the Occult and Supernatural* has defined Superstition as 'a form of personal magic used for coming to terms with the unknown . . . at the root of every superstition there lies a belief in magic . . .'

'You're doing a great job putting together something on our Westcountry superstitions,' a Cornishman said to me. 'Before long many of them will have been forgotten.'

He may have just been kind. Yet as I talk to people on the subject —though the interviews have all been here in Devon and Cornwall, the theme is surely international—I realised he is right. Many of them are fading from usage and memory.

But superstition curiously is not on its deathbed. Almost as if to contradict the disappearance of old expressions and little rituals, there is, in some quarters, a return to superstition. Maybe the empty pews in our churches and chapels have something to do with it.

Julie Welch, whose perceptive journalism regularly graces the pages of *The Observer*, a while back reflected: '. . . there is a feeling that the world is a pretty terrible place at the moment—that superstition is the panacea against its hideousness.'

Romany Reflections

Devon-born Acora is now acknowledged as one of the outstanding clairvoyants of the age. A Scorpio subject, he comes from a long line of travelling folk, and started making predictions at the age of seven.

'Seven,' he explained, 'is the most mystical number of all. My clairvoyancy has not been learnt from books or teachers . . . it's something I've inherited through blood and birth.'

This remarkable Romany soothsayer, whose predictions have won newspaper headlines and earned him TV and Radio broadcasts, had next to no schooling. 'Even today I prefer to read palms . . . and not words in a book!'

'Romanies are the genuine gypsies,' he reflected, 'a mysterious race of people who came from India centuries back in time. My great-grandmother, the celebrated Madam Zambra, had clients who included Royalty, and, not long ago, I was consulted by an Eastern Princess; so the tradition goes on.

'But the biggest influence in my life was my father's mother, Bessie Broadway. It was Gran who first recognised that I had the gift of second sight. I was about three or four, and the family were out in the country, somewhere in the wilds of Dartmoor. It was a hot summer's day and I wanted an ice-cream, but my father explained it was impossible in a place like that. "Go down the hill and turn right," I told him. Maybe just to keep me quiet, they went down the hill and turned right, and there, coming up the road, was an ice-cream van. Immediately my Grandmother knew I had the gift.'

Acora, in fact, spent a good deal of his childhood with his grand-mother, travelling the lanes and roads of Cornwall and Devon. 'In the winter months, we visited villages and isolated farms and cottages in the heart of the countryside, hawking things and, of course, telling fortunes. Gran always carried her crystal ball. In the summer, she followed the fairs and carnivals.'

We first talked in his consulting room at the Barbican—that picturesque old Elizabethan corner of Plymouth by the waterside—up a cobbled street, that conjures images of Drake and Raleigh, but is strangely called New Street. Later we continued our conversation in his caravan — *vardo* as the Romanies call it—in Cornwall. During the summer he and his wife Jeannette and their daughter Sammie travel great distances, following the Westcountry Fairs, like Corpus Christi at Penzance, Barnstaple Fair high up on the North Devon Coast, May Day at Padstow, right through to Goosie Fair at Tavistock in October.

'It was my Grandmother, too, who taught me something about the healing ways of the Romanies. You must remember that gypsies, in those days, had next to no education—so Romany knowledge was passed from generation to generation by word of mouth. I was lucky in the sense that she chose me as the one to receive her knowledge. So when we travelled the countryside on her hawking journeys, she would point out the plants and flowers, explaining too how according to ancient Romany lore they could be used for healing purposes. Interestingly Bessie's daughter—my aunt—is named Sante which, in Romanish, means "Health".

'As we wandered through the lanes and across country roads, Gran would educate me. She would perhaps point to the plant mandrake which is a subject of fiery Mars—as is the stinging nettle. Or she would explain that the cherry tree is the tree of lovers because it belongs to Venus, the planet of love. And, at night, over the camp fire she would teach me ancient recipes and remedies.'

Now our conversation moved on to the subject of superstition. Acora is convinced the tide of opinion has turned.

'There was a time when a lot of people treated superstition or the Supernatural as a laughing matter, but I suspect they're getting fewer and fewer. There's too much evidence pointing in the other direction.

'For example, there are certain folk who no longer regard the Curse of the Pharaohs as an empty threat. Ever since the Earl of Carnaervon discovered the tomb of Tutankhamen back in the 1920s,

Acora: ' . . . there's a very old gypsy tradition that a horse brings a traveller luck.' ▶

death has stalked those connected with the discovery.

' "Death shall come to him who touches the Tomb of Pharaoh," said the inscription over the door in the boy King's Tomb. Could that curse, from 3,000 years ago, still work its wicked will?

'Well, the first victim was the Earl himself who died just three weeks after breaking into the grave, dying from a fatal mosquito bite. Then an American archaeologist, staying in the same Cairo hotel, went into a coma and died. Even more incredibly, radiologist Douglas Reid, who X-rayed the body, came home to England, complained of exhaustion—and died. Within the space of six tragic calendars, thirteen of the twenty people present at the opening of the tomb died—and all before they had reached their sixtieth birthday.

'Some years ago a decision was made to move fifty relics of King Tutankhamen from Cairo to this country. The Doctor, who made the arrangements, said "I simply don't believe in the curse . . ." Four weeks after the signing of the agreement he was in his coffin—aged 52.

'Even more astonishing was how the curse struck the RAF crew who carried the mummified body of the King. As many as six members of that air crew have either died or suffered cruel illness.

'Working as I do in Occult matters, I would not treat that curse lightly—for the tragedies are too many to be just a chain of coincidences. The other side of the coin is where people come to me, asking me to unwind a bad influence—rather as people came to the old-fashioned white witches who removed warts and did healing. And I like to think that I use my gifts in the same positive way. It is interesting that we Romanies have practised prophecy down the ages. Despite the passing of centuries and the march of so-called progress, people still turn to us for predictions.

'I've always looked upon Egypt as the birthplace of superstition. The Romanies have long been linked with the land of pyramids. Just look at that word Egypt; cover the letter E and you've got *gypt!*

'Superstition is born into our Romany bones. For instance whenever I'm on a journey and meet a load of hay or straw, I always say *"Kooshti Bok!"* which, in Romanish, means "Good Luck!" We

Acora with his daughter Sammie: ▶
'During the summer they follow the Westcountry fairs . . .'

have an old saying which goes "See hay, money today. See straw, money to draw." In complete contrast, I never like to meet a hearse. In fact, some Romanies feel so strongly about it that if they see a hearse, they'll forget about business that day, turn round and go home.

'There are certain relations of the mice family—the bigger version —we never call them by their real name. That would be like opening the door to bad luck. Instead we refer to them as "long tails". A monkey is also considered unlucky. I remember visiting the fortune-teller Gypsy Lee, and telling her I had once owned a monkey. "That's it!" she said. She promptly closed the door and went home. She must have lost business that day, and I have always remembered never to use the word again in her company. Looking back on the time when I had that monkey I didn't have a lot of luck. Another thing we don't like to see is two nuns together. Two stopped outside my trailer on the fairground one day and I closed down. Things hadn't been going well, and I took those two nuns as an omen.

'I had a curious experience, last night. Jeannette and I were driving back to Cornwall. We had been invited to a dinner in Devon and I drove over a "long tail". That really upset me. Then five minutes later a black cat shot across the road in front of us. Fortunately I didn't hit him; so I consider that cancelled out the bad luck five minutes before.

'As I say, this superstition thing is bred into us. Laura, my mother-in-law, has just been offered a beautiful trailer at a ridiculously low price, but superstition's stopping her buying it. That caravan's almost new, but a man died in it. Well, that's considered an ill-omen by Romanies. Why, when my great-grandmother died, they burnt her caravan!

'Fire, of course, is one of the four elements and has always stood for purification and renewal, and fire magic is all linked up with superstition. I often find that staring into a fire does the same as when I'm peering into the crystal ball . . . I don't see pictures there but it clears my mind and helps me to pick up vibrations.

'And when Jeannette and I married, though we had a conventional church service, we also went through the Romany ritual of cutting our wrists . . . blood to blood . . . I've even the scars to this day.

'It's an old Romany tradition too that a gypsy woman who goes childless has been ill-wished. Non-Romanies would laugh about it, but we don't. For example, many people would say I'm silly to own a horse when I don't really need one. But there's a very old gypsy tradition that a horse brings a traveller luck. People, like Gypsies, Jews, and country folk, those who are closest to Mother Earth, are certainly more responsive to these old old traditions.'

Old Country Customs

Good Friday—for obvious reasons—is a day with strong superstitious links. In my lifetime I can recall fervent opposition to any pleasure-seeking on such a solemn day. The introduction of say football on Good Friday afternoon was seen by many as 'consorting with the Devil'. I can remember older relations declining to turn on the 'wireless', as it was called, on that special Friday, and music from a neighbouring house was regarded as almost an immoral act.

In olden days I gather farmers in the North Riding of Yorkshire would *never* dig, plough or harrow on Good Friday, believing it to be sacrilege to disturb the earth of the land on such a day of mourning. But this was not a universally accepted superstition or theory because in other parts of the country it was considered to be positively lucky to sow on Good Friday. In Devon, farmers felt that crops would 'come up goody' through Good Friday sowing, believing 'the better the day the better the deed'. Indeed some rose very early and did their sowing before dawn on Good Friday in the hope that things would grow at double their normal pace. Or did they perhaps rise so early to avoid incurring the wrath of others who took a narrow religious view about work on such a day? Today we can only guess.

Farm workers have long had a superstitious side to their character—inevitable perhaps due to working so close to nature. I remember an old lay preacher once telling me that some of the finest Christian characters he knew were men who worked the land. He firmly believed that their spiritual qualities owed a lot to Nature.

An interesting agricultural superstition was linked to the elm leaf; the notion being that the size of the elm leaf was a sure guide for the farmer's sowing of barley or the planting of kidney beans. Here are some old lines that former generations not only learnt by heart but apparently took seriously:

When the elm leaf is as big as a mouse's ear,
Then to sow barley never fear,
When the elm leaf is as big as an ox's eye,
Then say I 'Hie, bags Hie',
When elm leaves are as big as a shilling,
Plant kidney beans if to plant them you are willing,
When elm leaves are as big as a penny,
You must plant kidney beans if you mean to have any.

Here are some too for the broad bean:

One for the mouse,
One for the crow,
One for rot,
One to grow.

There was a sting in the tail here because it is said that if one of the beans came up white then there would be a death in the family during the year.

It would be impossible to make any journey among superstitions and not feel the influence of Twelfth Night. Here in the Westcountry it is a tradition among some villagers to go into their apple orchards on 17 January (Old Twelfth Night) to wassail the trees so they will bear plenty of fruit the following autumn. The word 'wassail' comes from the Old English phrase *wes hal* which means 'be of good health'.

Having selected one of the best trees in the orchard, the men fire their guns through the branches and sprinkle cider round the roots. In some places they soak a piece of cake or bread in cider, which they then place in a fork of the tree to placate the spirits who watch over the apple harvest. The following song is often sung before the wassailers retire to drink the rest of the cider:

Here's to thee, old apple tree,
Whence, thou mayst bud,
and when thou mayst blow,
And whence thou mayst bear apples enow!
Hats full, caps full!
And my pockets full, too!
Huzza! Huzza! Huzza!

Another version of this custom was known as 'Holow-ing to the

19

Appletrees'. Bread was toasted, treated in sugar and soaked in newly made cider. The mixture was heated and poured on the oldest tree in the orchard while everyone gathered round and sang:

> *Here's to thee,*   *Hatfulls, capfulls,*
> *Old apple tree,*   *Bushel, Bushel, Bossfulls,*
> *From every bough,*   *Hurrah Hurrah.*
> *Give us an apple enow,*

It is very sad how many of the old Westcountry customs have been allowed to die. In and around Okehampton, in the last century, for example, local children went 'Lent Crocking' on Shrove Tuesday each year. They chanted verses in and outside houses hoping to get gifts from the residents that would enable them to make their Shrove Tuesday pancakes. Eggs, flour and milk were given to the children as a kind of reward, and their chanting went like this:

> *LENT CROCK, give me a pancake,*
> *Or a fritter, for my labour,*
> *Or a dish of flour, or a piece of bread,*
> *Or what you please to render,*
> *I see by the latch,*
> *There is something to catch,*
> *I see by the string,*
> *There's a good dame within,*
> *Trap, trapping, throw,*
> *Give me my mumps and I'll be go!*

This ritual, amongst the youngsters, died out towards the end of the nineteenth century. 'Mumps' in the last line derived from the fact that 'a mumper' was a slang expression for a beggar, and in some parts of Devon, they drew their dole money on dates which were known as 'Mumping Days'.

Here is another simple rhyme used by dairymaids:

> *Come Butter, come,*
> *Come Butter, come,*
> *Peter stands by the gate,*
> *Waiting for a buttered cake,*

When the butter was slow in coming and requiring vigorous turning of the churns, the dairymaids cheered themselves with these lines.

A Cornish Bard Talks About Superstition

You can be mistaken about some people—even people you think you know pretty well—and I was mistaken over Joan Rendell.

Author and journalist, lecturer and traveller, Joan Rendell was made an MBE in 1958 and in 1977 she was awarded the Queen's Silver Jubilee Medal; while in 1980 she became a Bard of the Cornish Gorseth, taking the name of *Scryfer Weryn*—Writer of Werrington—where she has lived the greater part of her busy life.

Recognised as a world authority on matchbox labels, Joan Rendell's collection now exceeds 200,000, one of the biggest collections in the world. Some beautiful examples were clustered in a group near us. A fellow Bossiney author, she has written on subjects as diverse as the Bude Canal and Cornish Churches, Lundy and a history of her beloved Launceston.

A member of the Church of England and Secretary of the Launceston Old Cornwall Society, and of the Federation of Old Cornwall Societies, I never imagined she was superstitious. But with her Cornish ancestry—a St Austell father and a Helston mother—perhaps I should have guessed.

'I am very superstitious, always have been, something I inherited from my Cornish mother and aunt,' she explained. 'Ann, as I called my aunt, was with us all her life. She'd be more than a hundred if she were alive, and her superstitious nature rubbed off I suppose. In complete contrast, though, my father, a life-long Churchman, didn't believe in superstitions, dismissing them as "nonsense".

'I can still vividly remember my first superstition. Ann and I were out walking in the country, and, as a child, I loved picking flowers. I couldn't have been more than two years old, and I bent down to pick some dandelions. "Never pick dandelions; they'll make you wet the bed!" I can hear Ann's words all these years later. Then, about a year after that, we were in Scotland and I thought myself lucky to have found some lovely peacock feathers, but neither mother nor Ann would let me bring them into the house. "Keep them outside," they said. "If you bring them indoors they'll bring bad luck." Some time ago, I bought some peacock feathers for someone for a floral decoration, and when I brought them home, still remembering that advice all those years ago, I didn't bring them indoors. But after a day or two I weakened, thinking a mouse may be in the outhouse and might nibble away at those beautiful feathers. So indoors they came and almost immediately I had a nasty accident, injured by a falling ladder, and I still have the scar to this day. I shall always blame those blooming peacock feathers.'

We talked at Joan Rendell's home, just outside Launceston, on a February day 'lent' as we Cornish say, morning sunlight flooding the room and hinting at an early spring. 'I really believe in superstitions', she told me and she said the words with a quiet conviction. 'Superstition is a big part of my life. In fact it is a way of life.'

'Do you find any conflict with your religious beliefs?'

She laughed: 'No, but I suppose some people might think I'm an eccentric! It's all wrapped up with being Cornish. These superstitions have been handed down the generations. It's almost something born in your blood.'

'You've had other genuine experiences of superstitions coming true then!'

'Oh, yes, many, many instances.

'Take for example, a robin coming into the house. That's an omen of death. I remember Ann lying in bed and discovering a robin fluttering around her bedroom. "That's the end of me!" she said, and it was. She died within a few days of the robin coming indoors.

'And I had a very recent experience. For some curious reason, I found that my loaves of bread had holes in them, not just once but several times running. I didn't like that, and I told the baker so. That's a sign of death, but they laughed it off. Well, only last weekend I heard suddenly that an old family friend had just died.

'More people are superstitious than they'll often admit in public. Recently I was at a committee meeting, and thirteen of us turned up. That's reputed to be a bad number, and one of our members, a

Joan Rendell: 'Superstition is a big part of my life. In fact it is a way of life. . .all wrapped up with being Cornish. . .' ▶

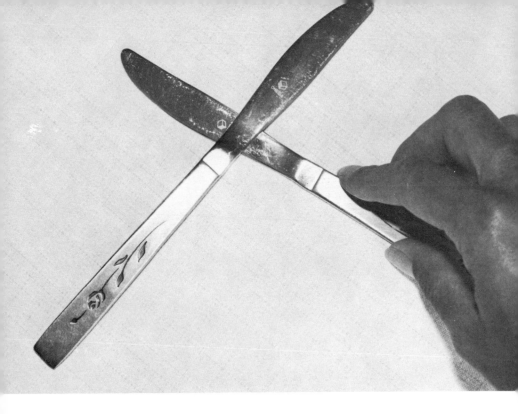

highly respected man in the community, wanted to leave the meeting and go home, simply because we were an unlucky thirteen. However, we persuaded him to stay. But he didn't sit around the table. He sat quite apart from us so that it wouldn't be a case of thirteen around the table that evening.

'A lot of people treat superstitions very seriously, and though they may not like to acknowledge the fact it's basically a pagan religion.'

I remembered too that Joan Rendell is an expert on Corn Dollies and has written an excellent book on the subject for Faber and Faber.

'Corn Dollies are essentially symbols,' she explained, 'to encourage the fertility of crops. Primitive people wanted to preserve the corn spirit, wanting it to remain alive and active through the coming calendar. We believe the making of corn dollies began in ancient Egypt, where they made crude effigies of the human body, and sometimes buried them in tombs with their Gods.'

Left: '. . . a robin coming into the house. That's an omen of death.'
Far left: 'If the knives cross, that's another superstition linked to death.'

'But here in Cornwall and other places where cereals are grown the old custom is to keep plaited heads and stalks of corn from the last sheaf cut at harvest time. In Cornwall, the ritual's called "crying the nek".'

Inevitably our conversation turned to colours. 'If you wear green, you'll wear black. That's another old superstition. I *never* wear green.' She said that word *never* with a finality, no room for perhaps or maybe. 'And you'll never find me driving a green car either. My mother wore green to a wedding and almost immediately after my grandmother died. Mother always blamed that green dress for the death.

'Something else I'd never do is go back to a house, where I had lived before . . . you'd die!

'The crossing of knives is also bad. If the knives cross, that's another superstition linked to death. I shall always remember being on holiday with a friend in Sweden, and as we sat down to have a meal in the dining room of this hotel, my friend knocked the cutlery

25

in such a way that two knives crossed. "That's a sign of death!" I blurted out. "Don't say that, Joan," she said, and shortly after returning home her husband departed this life.'

'Isn't there a danger that superstitions can turn you into a negative character?' I asked.

'Yes, I think that sometimes. I often think the worst because I am so superstitious by nature ... you're probably right, one ought to be more positive and concentrate on the good superstitions ... things like spitting on a coin for luck and putting a wish on a black cat.'

So we ended our conversation on a positive note, and as I drove back along the narrow winding North Cornwall lanes, I realised talking to Joan Rendell had been an enlightening experience. I'd not only encountered some new superstitions and gained some genuine first-hand experiences, I was now seeing her in a new light, and even the day in a curious way confirmed that fact. I hadn't seen a bluer sky for weeks.

Some Devon Folklore

Romance and superstition seem to have been linked for a long, long time too. One old Devon rhyme goes:

> *An even leafed ash,*
> *And a four-leafed clover,*
> *You see your true love*
> *Ere the day is over.*

In Okehampton though the young folk had a more down-to-earth method of finding a partner. This custom was known as Giglet Market and fell on the Saturday following Christmas, when the young men of the town had the privilege of *self-introduction* to any young lady, provided, of course, she was a spinster. This act of self-introduction was given official approval in that an old Charter of Okehampton granted the privilege. The young ladies naturally dressed smartly in the hope of attracting attention, and the seeds of many happy romances were sown. Sadly though the custom died out.

On the Moor above Okehampton, adjacent to the road to the Army Camp, is a granite cross marking an old well, Fitz's Well, which also has a strong romantic tradition. At Easter any young woman, seeking a suitable husband, came here, early in the morning, to drink from the well on Easter Day. The local tradition was that if she came early and sipped the water of Fitz's Well, she would be married within twelve months.

Then another romantic belief concerned Midsummer Day. On that date in the calendar, the Devon maid, without a potential husband, would pluck a rose and wrap it in paper. Then on Christmas morning she would wear it to Church in the hope that a young man would take it from her—and thereby pave the way to a happy marriage.

Devon also had a curious wedding door ceremony relating to the

27

marriage of a younger daughter. If an elder sister was unmarried, then after the marriage ceremony, a small faggot, made of furze, was placed across the threshold of the bride's home. There was this old notion that a younger sister marrying before an older one would cast a spell of bad luck. However this spell could be broken by the elder unmarried girl stepping over the faggot on her return to the house. By stepping over the faggot, she was overcoming the obstacle to her marriage and the curious old custom was known as 'dancing the furze faggot'.

★ ★ ★

Devon keeps alive some ancient traditions. Ashburton, one of Dartmoor's gateways, is such a case.

Once a year, on 26 November, a ceremony is acted out in the town of Ashburton which dates back to the time of King Alfred. At a special court, known as a court leet, a local citizen is elected to the ancient office of Portreeve for the following year. Nowadays the Portreeve is merely a figurehead, but originally he was the equivalent of our modern mayor. The court leet is held in the chapel of St Lawrence, which was founded in 1314 as a school and chantry. At the same time the court elects a number of other traditional and unusual posts; that of Ale Taster, Bread Weigher, Pig Driver, Scavenger and Surveyors of Markets and Water Courses.

On the Thursday of Carnival Week, which is held in Ashburton at the end of June or beginning of July, the Ale Taster, together with the Portreeve and other officials, visits all the inns in the town to taste the beer and check on its quality. Originally, when about forty establishments in the town were brewing their own beer, it was to ensure that clean water and the right ingredients were being used. If the beer is deemed to be of acceptable quality, the Portreeve presents the landlord with a spray of evergreen to hang over his door. Then the officials visit the two bakeries in the town to weigh the bread using an ancient pair of bread scales which are kept in the museum and taken out once a year for this purpose.

★ ★ ★

◄Author, Michael Williams

Hereabouts, we need to clarify one area of folklore and I'm indebted to Mrs Bray of Tavıstock in her *Traditions of Devonshire* for such clarification.

Pixies are not to be confused with fairies, as they are a quite separate race. The country folk used to say that pixies were the souls of infants who had died before they could be baptized. These little people are always dressed in green and delight in dancing, which they always do in a ring or circle. Each pixie is given a special task by the king of the pixies, some good, some mischievous, such as leading travellers astray, playing practical jokes, making sure housewives have done their cleaning properly. People used to place a basin of water by the chimney nook, as pixies loved water.

Here is an example of their darker side—of a man being pixy-led and the seeds of tragedy being sown. To the south of the churchyard in Combe Martin was a group of old oak trees which used to be part of the parkland surrounding the castle of Combe Martin, of which very little remains. There is a rather poignant story explaining how the castle fell into ruins, which runs as follows.

The last lord of the manor had an only son, whom he loved dearly. This son was passionately fond of stag hunting, and often used to spend long days on Exmoor, hunting with his pack of hounds. One morning in autumn he left as usual at dawn, telling the porter he did not intend going very far, and would be back before dark. There was a deep moat surrounding the castle, and it was the porter's duty to raise the drawbridge every evening when night fell.

Dusk came, and in spite of his promise, the lord's son did not return. The porter waited until long after dark, but still there was no sign of him, and at length, the porter decided that the young man must have strayed further than he intended, and had been forced to shelter elsewhere for the night. So he reluctantly raised the drawbridge and closed the castle gates.

The night was very dark and windy, and there was no moon. Some time later the young man came riding up the road to the castle, he and his dogs very weary after their long day. He could see nothing in the pitch dark, but he knew the road well, and as he drew near the castle he spurred his horse on, anxious to be home. Suddenly the horse stopped, frightened, but the lord's son urged him on impatiently. The horse leapt forward, there was a sudden cry, a splash, and then silence as the cold waters of the moat closed over them both. When the lord of the manor learned what had happened he was

'Cats have long featured in the realm of Superstition.'

so heartbroken he could not bear to stay in the castle, so he abandoned it and went abroad, and the castle fell into ruin, a monument to the darker side of the pixies.

★　　★　　★

Cats have long featured in the realm of superstition.

If a cat sleeps on his brain
It is a sure sign of rain.

That ancient couplet is only one example of a cat's alleged clairvoyancy. Another tradition is that if the cat sits with his or her back to the fire it is an indication that cold weather is on the way.

Country families never liked kittens in the house at the same time as a new baby; the old belief being that a kitten would harm the child. But, on other occasions, a cat would be most welcome. If, for instance, thirteen people sat down to dinner then a cat would be placed in the lap of one of the diners, thereby ensuring that fourteen and not the unlucky thirteen, sat around the table. Moreover the

31

presence of a black cat, on such an occasion, was said to confer good luck on the thirteen human diners.

Michael Wreford told me an interesting Dartmoor tale about some kittens. The tale was told to him first-hand by an old Dartmoor man. He was farming on the Moor around the turn of the century, and the cat of the house gave birth to three kittens—an event that gave great pleasure to the children in the family—but the housekeeper refused to stay if the kittens remained under the roof. The animals were born in the month of May, and the superstitious housekeeper claimed that May cats were notorious for bringing into the house 'varmints'—unwelcome animals. She maintained that she had had experience of this feline habit in her previous place of employment, and it became a case of 'Either those May kittens go or I go!'

★   ★   ★

Some of the old Devon cures for children have a positively barbaric ring. Two particularly unpleasant traditions related to whooping cough. The first was for the unfortunate child to wear a bag around his or her neck containing a caterpillar, preferably a long-haired one; while the second meant an early rise for the patient by taking the child to a field and laying the child, face down, dew on the ground, where a sheep had just been lying.

Even more arduous but perhaps less unpleasant was for the mother to take her coughing child to three different parishes in one day—and this belief stems from pre-motor car days when shanks's pony would probably have been the order of the day. Alternatives were to place a smooth mullein leaf under the left foot of the patient—or to inhale the breath of a horse.

Even more barbaric though was a preventive act. The baby or child would be taken by its parents to a freshly prepared grave—a grave dug for the body of the opposite sex—and the child then would be placed in the grave for a few moments to 'ensure that the child would not be susceptible to illnesses prevalent in other children'. One wonders what the NSPCC would say about that today—or child psychologists.

Whooping cough seems to have especially generated countryside superstitions. One old belief is that if a girl married and retained the first letter of her surname—that's to say her married surname began with the same letter as her maiden name—she would be unlucky. An exception to her unlucky pattern though was the belief that any sick children could be brought to her and something she cooked would cure them.

Another unpleasant cure for whooping cough was to take a hair from the head of the affected child and put it inside a bread and butter sandwich—and give this curious sandwich to a dog. If the dog coughed, then the child would be cured. One wonders what the RSPCA and Barbara Woodhouse would say about that too.

Times were when collecting sticks was an important part of a working family's life because sticks for an open fire were a vital factor in cooking and keeping a cottage warm. But it was considered very unlucky to pick up sticks on the Sabbath. 'If you collect sticks on Sunday,' the old folk said, 'you'll go to the moon.' The notion behind this was two-fold: first, respectable people rested on 'The Lord's Day' and kept it 'holy', and secondly that only witches collected sticks for their broomsticks on a Sunday.

The devious adults though would send their children out on a Sunday to scout for wood. The children would get the sticks together in some suitably concealed spot, and then go out on Monday and bring them in.

On the subject of 'keeping Sunday holy', this is a tradition that clung long to us here in the Westcountry. Only thirty years ago, I recall the son of a Non-Conformist being told by his local preacher father: 'If you go to that dance on Saturday evening . . . make sure you're out of the dance hall before midnight . . . keep the Sabbath holy.'

★ ★ ★

There was a remarkable scene in a North Devon Church on Sunday 15 April 1906. The Reverend F.G. Scrivenor the Rector of Sutcombe wrote a report of what took place:

'North Devon is full of strange folklore and beliefs. On Sunday the Parish Church of Sutcombe, a small village between Holsworthy and Hartland, was the scene of a revival of an old cure. A woman in the parish has of late been a sufferer of epileptic fits, and at the persuasion of a neighbour who nineteen years ago had done the same thing, and had not suffered from fits since, she went around the parish and got thirty married men to promise to attend the

33

parish Church at the morning service. It was gratifying to see so many people in the congregation, all drawn together out of sympathy for a neighbour and a desire to do anything that they thought might help her. At the close of the service the rector desired the selected men to pass out one by one and as they passed through the Porch, they found the woman seated there, accompanied by the neighbour who had done the same thing nineteen years ago—as many who were present remembered. Each man, as he passed out, put a penny in the woman's lap, but when the thirtieth man—the Rector's churchwarden—came he took the 29 pennies and put in half a crown. A silver ring is to be made of the half crown, which the woman is to wear and it is hoped that the result will be as satisfactory in her case as it was on the previous occasion. In a small parish—less than 300 population—it was not easy to find thirty men married, but all were willing to help—farmers, labourers, and tradesmen, and the whole incident passed off very quietly, and all was done with the utmost decorum and reverence. The woman takes her seat in the Porch when the preacher begins his service, and from the time she leaves her house until she returns home she must not speak a word.'

The Rector went on to say that he would be interested to hear details of any similar case, and he received a very quick and interesting reply. It came from the Reverend Roger Granville, who wrote in similar vein about an occurrence in 1891, when he had been Rector of Bideford. He wrote:

'Some fifteen years ago when I was Rector of Bideford, a young woman suffering from epileptic fits asked me to go to the Porch after preaching and hold her hand while she collected a penny from thirty married men as they passed out of the Church the following Sunday evening, which thirty coppers were to be exchanged for a silver half crown out of which a ring was to be made which she would wear and so be cured of epilepsy.

'I feel I was not so complacent as the Rector of Sutcombe and declined to foster such superstition as I regarded it. The woman ceased in consequence to be a member of the Church of England, and joined the Wesleyan body. I do not remember hearing that she was any more successful with them though. On another occasion a young farmer from the neighbourhood of Torrington called on me and asked me what was contained in a bag he had worn round his neck since infancy and which a white witch had given his mother as

34

a preventative against epilepsy. After cutting open several cases well worn with sweat and stains, I came upon the original inner one, which contained a number of pieces of paper each bearing a word. Piecing them together, I found they formed the following sentences: 'Sinner, Jesus died for thee'—thrice repeated—'Therefor flee that sin.' At the man's request these pieces were reinserted in their several bags and my maidservant sewed them up again, and he, replacing them around his neck, once more went on his way rejoicing, being now in a position to tell his neighbour whose child also had fits, that there was a certain cure for them.'

Today the term is 'fringe medicine' or 'alternative medicine' but, in fact, cures, outside conventional medical practice, have been with us a long, long time. Down the ages, men and women have passed on remedies and cures from one generation to another.

Women, 'wise women', were especially looked upon as local experts by those seeking a cure in days when 'National Health' was not even a dream. Today, one suspects, many of them would generate snorts of derision from the medical profession — and from the Church too perhaps because, in a few instances, there was a tenuous link with the Devil himself.

For example, a Devon remedy for St Vitus Dance was for the patient or victim to wear an amulet which carried these words:

> *Shake her good Devil,*
> *Shake her once well,*
> *Then shake her no more,*
> *Till you shake her in hell!*

Here is another Devon cure for boils: 'Go into a Churchyard on a dark night and to the grave of a person who has been interred the previous day. Walk around the grave six times, and crawl across it three times. If the sufferer be a man, this ceremony must be performed by a woman and vice versa. Be warned this act will not work unless the night is dark.'

Another old Moorland remedy for toothache involved a visit to the Church, this time to find a skull, and then take a tooth from the skull and carry it around with you. People, who suffered from cramps, had to remove old coffin handles from a grave and make them into rings—in fact any metal work from the coffin is thought to do the trick.

Frankly I wouldn't care to have tried either of those methods. I would though have tried another Devon variation associated with toothache. This entailed going to that lovely winding Westcountry river, the Teign, which begins life high on Dartmoor and ends it by the sea at Teignmouth. This pattern brought echoes from the Men-an-Tol down in West Cornwall because the Devon version too is to seek the holed stone in the Teign near its junction with Walla Brook.

It was Colin Heald, a former Governor of Dartmoor Prison, who introduced me to the delights of Hedge's snuff, and I was therefore interested to hear of a famous Okehampton musician who maintained that mental illness could be averted by the taking of snuff. His duties, in the last century, included the unhappy business of taking mental patients to the County Asylum—as it was called in those days—and he claimed that he never escorted a patient who was a 'snuff taker'. That's quite a claim, so maybe snuff does 'clear the head' in a medical sense.

As someone who enjoys a glass of wine, I was also fascinated by another cure from east of the Tamar: this time relating to the pains of rheumatism. The prescription is to drink a glass of white wine on rising and another on retiring at night. But this ancient Devon 'medicine' requires the following ingredients.

As Mrs Beeton might have put it: 'Take one ounce of sulphur, one ounce of cream of tartar, one drachm of gum guiacum, half an ounce of rhubarb together with sixteen ounces of honey.' This should be thoroughly mixed together and the mixture stored for use as required. A tablespoon of the concoction should then be added to the white wine, and very hot water.

★　　★　　★

Times were when I saw fact and fiction as black and white, living inside clearly defined boundaries. Yet the older I get, the less sure I am whether there can be such a thing as total myth. Once upon a time, I thought King Arthur and the Court of Camelot existed only inside the pages of legend—and within imagination—but having

A weather omen: 'If the ash comes out before the oak there'll be a soak. If the oak comes out before the ash there'll be a splash.' ▶

met members of a psycho-expansion group who claim to have been Arthurian characters in a previous existence, that belief has been exploded.

Here in Devon the Doones have fascinated for years.

Though the notorious Doones were based on Exmoor in Somerset, it is impossible to ignore them in Devon folklore for the plain fact is they committed many of their wicked deeds inside the Devon borders.

One theory is that the clan, originally Scottish free-booters, came to Bagworthy in the days of Cromwell and soon acquired a terrible reputation for miles around, terrorising, murdering and blackmailing.

North Devon poet and farmer, Ronald Duncan, believed there is considerable evidence to suggest R.D. Blackmore based his famous novel *Lorna Doone,* first published in 1869, *on fact.*

Back in 1901, a lady, named Audrey Doon, wrote a feature in *The West Somerset Free Press* which made certain claims. First, she claimed to be a member of the original Doone family, and went on to reveal that Sir Ensor Doone, the Robber Chief in Blackmore's novel, was the twin brother of the Earl of Moray, who was banished from Doune Castle in Perthshire because of family quarrels. Failing to obtain redress, Sir Ensor headed for the Westcountry, abandoning land and fortune. She further claimed that Sir Ensor and his wife and a servant settled in a farm in the East Lyn Valley, quite near Oare Ford. Miss Doon, in that 1901 article, quoted from a diary kept by one of her family in the eighteenth century.

> 1747 Sept. 3rd. Went to Barum on my way to the place they call Oare, whence our people came after their cruel treatment by the Earl of Moray.
> Sept. 7th. Got to Oare and then to the valley of the Lyn. The scenery very bonny like our own land, but the part extremely wild and lonely. Wandered about and thought of the old days of the family there, which I gathered were not peacable.

You have only to look at the wild terrain of Exmoor and parts of North Devon, remembering how desolate it would have been 250 years ago, to realize the existence of such a band of rogues was perfectly feasible.

One of my favourite folklore figures is Tom Faggus, the debonair

Highwayman who is such a character in *Lorna Doone*. I never come over Barnstaple Bridge without thinking of him. On one occasion, Faggus riding his 'enchanted strawberry horse', found himself cut off on the bridge; parties of men, pursuing him, blocked both extremities. But to the astonishment of both parties, the horse, bearing Tom Faggus, cleared the parapet and swam away to safety. Old folk told how Tom became a Highwayman. Apparently he was the blacksmith of North Molton, but had the misfortune to lose all he possessed in a disastrous lawsuit. Giving up his craft of blacksmith, he became a 'gentleman adventurer'. Living frugally himself, he plundered the rich without mercy and gave generously to the poor and sick. There is an almost Arthurian quality about him, and I, for one, like to think the Tom Faggus of Blackmore's imagination *did* in fact originate from a real character.

Superstition in Sport

Sport has some superstitions too.

Rugger players are usually rated pretty down-to-earth types, but I have seen a Rugby XV contain a number 16 jersey, the club declining to ask someone to wear the 13th. I have also known cricketers and footballers — of both codes — who favoured being the last man to go onto the field. I recall one experienced county player, who would make all sorts of excuses, to ensure he was the last man to leave the dressing room.

Cricket, very much an Establishment game in many eyes, perhaps surprisingly has its share of superstitious characters. Derek Pringle, the young England cricketer, for instance, makes a circle around the stumps when he comes in to bat, while Australian Mike Whitney admits he kisses the ball when he is about to begin a spell of bowling.

Here in Cornish cricket, one experienced opening batsman, a man who has captained his county, kisses his bat every time he scores a boundary; another experienced campaigner always rates a break for 'drinks' in hot weather a favourable omen for the toiling bowlers —and it *is* interesting that a wicket often does fall immediately after the refreshments. This, though, could be psychological because at Lords it was often said members of the Royal Family did well for England, after the Royal presentation a wicket invariably falling.

Some cricketers too dislike cleaning their pads when they're enjoying a 'scoring run'. Greg Chappell, the Australian, for example, on a tour of England refused to clean his pads for weeks, presumably believing that whitening his pads would wash away his batting form. And cricketers everywhere dread 'The Lord Nelson'. This cricketing 'curse' is when the scoreboard stands at 111 — the three ones. Time and time again, a batsman gets out with the score board reading that ominous number. The expression 'The Lord

A dreaded 'Lord Nelson' at cricket: the
scoreboard reading 111.

Nelson' is due to the fact that the famous Admiral had one eye, one
arm and one 'unmentionable piece of anatomy'. Denis Compton, on
one indiscreet broadcasting occasion, was on the verge of
mentioning the unmentionable when he was silenced by a senior
colleague! The fact remains most batting sides dislike the
appearance of those three figures, and heave a sigh of relief when
the score moves on.

Omens

Acorn: Carrying an acorn in your pocket is supposed to keep you looking youthful, though it works better for women than for men. This probably comes from the old Druid belief that the oak tree was sacred and had special powers.

Ashes: Used worldwide as a fertility charm. Ashes from special fires, such as those lit on Midsummer's night, are spread on crops to ensure a good harvest.

Badger: Gamblers believe that badgers bring them luck — if you keep a badger's tooth in your pocket, you should never lose a wager.

Bats: Many people are rather frightened of bats, and for this reason they have come to be regarded as a harbinger of bad luck. Better beware if a bat flies near you, as this means someone is trying to bewitch you.

Bells: Throughout Europe it is believed that ringing the church bells will drive away evil spirits, and if rung during a storm, will cause the rough weather to become calm.

Bird: A bird dropping his 'visiting card' on you is extremely lucky.

Blackberries: Never to eat blackberries after the 30th day of September is an ancient country custom. 'After that day,' they'd say, 'the Devil is inside the blackberries!' In the south-west it was also believed that a good blackberry season indicated a good herring season to come.

Bones: Never burn bones or you'll hear groans.

Breakages: To break a mirror means seven years bad luck. To break a bottle is also bad luck but not to the same extent. Gypsies, however, believe that to break some valuable crockery is good because if you hadn't broken it, something more precious — in life — would have been broken. Furthermore if you break anything of value, break a matchstick into three pieces as this will prevent further breakages.

Bridge: It is very unlucky to say goodbye to a friend on a bridge, because if you do, you will never meet him again. It is also

'It is unlucky to say goodbye to a friend on a bridge.'

unlucky to pass under a railway bridge if a train is going overhead. However it is lucky to go over a bridge if the train is passing under.

Burial: The old gypsies believed you should be buried where you were born — your grave should be in the village or town where you first saw the light of day.

Burning: To burn ivy, holly, elder or anything green is to invite ill luck.

Candle: A candle can be used to predict the future in various ways: if it is reluctant to light, then a storm is on the way; if it gutters in a room where there are no draughts, bad weather is imminent. If the candle flame burns blue, it foretells a frost, or even a death. On important occasions, such as births, marriages or deaths, lighting candles will ward off evil spirits.

Cats: A black cat crossing your path is an especially good sign — and you should put a wish on the cat. But a white cat has been traditionally considered unlucky.

43

'To burn holly and ivy
or anything green is to invite ill luck.'

Charming: The evidence of charming — like the evidence of ghosts — is overwhelming. Thousands of people have had warts removed by charmers — there have been cases of charming curing shingles too. But many charmers never like the patient to say 'Thank You'. They fear that somehow this usual courtesy will unwind the good work of the charming.

Chimney Sweep: A bride who meets and kisses a chimney sweep on her way out of church will have good luck and happiness for the rest of her life. The story goes that before his marriage to the Queen in 1947, Prince Philip caught sight of a sweep in the road outside Buckingham Palace, and rushed outside to shake hands with him.

Christmas Decorations: Remove all Christmas decorations on the 6 January as it is unlucky to keep them up beyond that date.

Clover: To find a four-leafed clover without looking for it is another good omen.

Coal: Because coal symbolises fire and warmth, it is considered lucky. In the past, people would carry a small piece of coal in their pockets to protect them from ill luck. It is still carried by First Footers on New Year's Eve. It used to be considered lucky to find a piece of coal on the road, though in some places you had to spit on it and throw the coal over your left shoulder and not look back. A lump of coal found on a beach would be given to a sailor as a protection against drowning.

Cock Crowing: When a cock crows on the stroke of midnight, this means a member of the household will soon depart this Life. On the subject of death, there is an ancient Westcountry theory that a man or woman cannot depart from this Life easily if his or her bed is made of fowl's feathers — or the feathers of wild birds.

Coffee: Americans believe that you can tell the future by studying the bubbles on the surface of a cup of coffee — bubbles coming towards you indicate that money will come your way, but bubbles floating away from you mean hard times ahead.

Coffin: Bad luck for a mourning family if the coffin containing the corpse is taken along a newly-made road. Many Romanies interpret the sight of a hearse on a journey as an omen that things will go badly that day.

Cornish Chough: With his glossy black plumage, scarlet legs and long curved scarlet beak, the chough is more than a mere bird to the patriotic Cornish. He is the symbol of Cornwall. According to legend, when the Cornish Chough goes, Cornwall's prosperity will go with him. Superstition however provides a ray of hope because deep back in Cornish folklore is a notion Arthur did not die in battle. Instead the Chough incarnated the King's soul — and Arthur will come again.

Cuckoo: It is a bad omen to hear a cuckoo call after the last day of July.

Cup of Tea: To pour an extra cup of tea — by mistake — foretells the coming of an unwelcome visitor.

Curlew: When you hear a curlew cry the weather will be hot.

Cutting Hair:

> *Best never enjoyed if Sunday shorn,*
> *And likewise leave out Monday.*
> *Cut Thursday and you'll never grow rich,*
> *Likewise on a Saturday.*
> *But live long if shorn on a Tuesday,*
> *And best of all is Friday.*

'A candle can be used to predict the future.'

(Strangely enough, my barber, Peter Prior, at Camelford, who has been cutting hair for forty years, hadn't heard of the haircutting superstition, and he assured me that it wasn't a tactical admission to ensure he didn't lose business on certain days. 'In the heyday of hairdressing,' he recalled, 'when the men had their hair cut, at least, once a month, Saturday was the busiest day of the week for barbers — simply because most of his customers were at work the other days.'

During the conversation at Camelford, another customer, waiting his turn, declared he had believed in the power of the gypsy's curse all his life. 'My brother was a robust boy of two and a half. Well, one day, a gypsy called at the house selling things. My brother, very young and not knowing better, tipped the gypsy's wares all over the doorstep. The gypsy, furious with anger, unleashed a string of curses, and my brother died within six months. Mother always put it down to the gypsy's curse.')

Dog: An old rural notion was 'Gain a dog, gain a friend'.

Donkey: To hear a donkey bray means rain before the end of the day.

Dress: It is bad luck to put your left arm first into your clothes when getting dressed, because the left is associated with the devil. If you do up your buttonholes wrongly it is also bad luck unless you undo them immediately and do them up correctly. On the other hand it is lucky to put on an article of clothing inside out — though you must leave it like that all day!

Dropping: To drop a glove or a comb indicates a pleasant surprise for the person who picks it up — but bad luck if the owner picks it up. The dropping of a spoon however has another interpretation in that it is said to forecast a stranger coming to the door.

Ebony Elephants: Always turn the elephants to face the door for good luck.

Eggshells: Never burn eggshells as this act will bring bad luck.

Left: An old rural notion was 'gain a Dog, gain a friend'.
Below: 'To hear a donkey bray means rain before the end of day.'

Elbow: An itching elbow means that you will soon be sleeping in a strange bed. If you knock your elbow it is bad luck, unless you then bang the other one as well. If you bite your elbow while thinking of someone you dislike, that person will be drenched in a storm — but have you tried biting your elbow?

Elder Tree: An elder tree in a garden or the grounds was thought to keep evil spirits at bay.

Feather: If you see a black feather in a field, stick it into the ground and make a wish.

Fire: A fire burning blue is a sign of frost.

First Footing: In the old days in Cornwall, it was considered very bad luck if a female were first to enter a house on New Year's Morning. Consequently the gentry usually instructed a man servant to perform the necessary first footing. In some Westcountry districts too it was thought a lucky ritual to sand your doorstep at the beginning of a new calendar.

Fish: Eat a fish from the tail upwards to ensure a good catch the next time out.

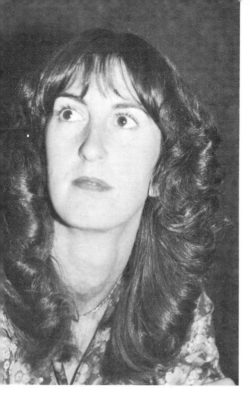

Far Left: 'The appearance of gulls inland is the sign of stormy weather.'

Left: 'Dark has always been considered the luckiest hair. . .'

Forgetting: If you leave the house and have to go back for something forgotten, sit down before going out again as this will avoid ill luck.

Fox: To see a lone fox means good luck, though to see several is a bad omen. If a fox is seen lurking near a house, it is a sign of impending disaster, or even of death.

Friday: Never start a venture or a new job on a Friday or it will not prosper.

Gloves: An old Romany belief is that when presenting glcves as a gift you must receive something in exchange.

Grass: If a cat or dog is seen eating grass, then rain is on the way.

Gulls: The appearance of gulls inland is the sign of stormy weather.

Hair: Human hair has generated a variety of superstitions. A good measure of hair, for example, has always been associated with strength. A life of riches was usually prophesied for a young man with hairy arms. The sudden loss of hair, during an illness, was said to be indicative of the death of a loved one. Curly hair was believed to reflect a contented nature, and dark hair has always been considered the luckiest hair, especially when related to 'First Footers' entering a house at the beginning of a New Year. But there has always been a doubt about people with red hair, and this probably has its origins in Biblical times as Judas Iscariot, who betrayed Christ, had red hair. But another British version is that the prejudice stems from the red-headed Danish pirates who long ago infested the British coastline.

Handkerchief: Don't put a folded handkerchief in your pocket. In the case of a young man this means he will not marry. But the handkerchief can counteract. If, for instance, your left ear burns someone is abusing you or spreading gossip — then tie a knot in your handkerchief and you will make the 'gossip' bite his tongue.

Hat: If you put your hat on back to front, you will have a day of bad luck, unless you cancel it by buying a new one.

Hawthorn: It is unlucky to bring hawthorn indoors — also lilac.

Hearse: Despite the dread Romany reaction to a hearse, a non-Romany superstition is that to meet a hearse coming towards you is lucky — but one going in the same direction is unlucky.

Heather: To find a piece of white heather is counted very lucky.

Horses: Horse shoes and horse brasses top the popularity stakes in the field of charms. They have long been regarded as extremely lucky as the horse has natural links with iron, a magical metal, worked by fire, a mysterious element. Moreover finding a horse shoe is rated a lucky event. There must be thousands of doors that bear a horse shoe. Admiral Lord Nelson is reputed to have nailed one to the mainmast of his HMS *Victory.* Down the centuries the horse shoe is believed to have contained Supernatural powers, possibly a legacy of pagan horse worship. In times past too horse brasses were reckoned more than stylish ornaments, they were considered amulets, protecting the animal from the influence of the Evil Eye. It's an old country tradition that horses are particularly vulnerable to witchcraft. The Romany folk have always regarded the white horse as a particularly good omen. While they also like to see a piebald because according to age-old gypsy tradition, you should then put a wish on the piebald.

Horse Shoes: '. . . extremely lucky as the horse has
natural links with iron, a magical metal.' ▶

Ink Spot: It is lucky to spill ink onto the paper when writing a letter.

Innocents Day: Never wash clothes on Innocents Day — or there will be a death in the family.

Inside Out: An article of clothing put on inside out should not be changed until after midday — this also indicates that a gift is in the offing.

Iron: If the iron drops to the floor when you are ironing the clothes someone will leave the home before the year is out. Another omen is that when opening a freshly ironed article, if a diamond shaped crease appears in the centre then this predicts a wedding in the family.

Itching: Itching in the centre of your hand indicates money coming to you. While the bottom of your foot itching is a sign that you will soon be walking on strange ground.

Knife and Fork: If a knife falls to the ground, a strange woman will visit you. If a fork falls, a strange man will call. The crossing of knives is especially unlucky — some superstitious folk interpreted the crossing as an omen of death. One theory is that the bad luck can be averted by gently removing the lower knife first.

Ladder: Walking under a ladder is unlucky.

Ladybird: To see a ladybird is lucky - therefore never kill it.

Leap Year: A leap year is always an auspicious one for important undertakings. Anything begun on 29 February is sure to turn out well. It is quite acceptable for women to propose to men during a leap year, though in Scotland girls had to wear a scarlet petticoat, which had to be visible, when proposing — could this be the origin of the term 'scarlet woman'?

Lucky Find: To find a farthing is a good omen — so much so they were carried in the purse for good luck.

March: There is an old country saying that a wet March makes for a bad harvest; a dry and cold March will never beg its bread.

Marriage: Sit on a table and you'll not marry that year. If you're a bridesmaid three times, you'll never be a bride.

May: Never whitewash in May because it brings bad luck.

Milk: It is a good omen to see milk when first waking up in the

'Romany folk have always regarded the white horse as a particularly good omen.' ▶

morning but spilling milk should be avoided at all costs, because milk is the favourite drink for fairies who will move into any house where milk has been spilt on the floor.

Money on Monday: Some of the old-fashioned travellers say: 'Never pay out on Monday or you'll pay out all week.'

Mountain-Ash: The mountain-ash has a very powerful reputation among country folk who believe it is capable of curing ills, whether those be natural or supernatural. The mountain-ash can unwind the spell of a witch. In olden times if a cow fell ill, the farmer would go to the nearest mountain-ash, also called *care*, and would bring branches from the tree and hang them over the cow's stall or wrap them around the animal's horns.

Nails: Never cut finger or toe nails on a Friday or a Sunday.

Nests: Rooks building their nests high in the trees indicate that a fine summer is coming.

New Moon: To see the new moon through glass has long been considered very unlucky, but to see it in the open air is a good omen, especially if seen over your right shoulder. According to a Westcountry 'wise woman' you should bow three times to the moon, and turn over any silver coins in your pocket. There is an ancient superstition too that any new venture begun on the first day of a new moon will prosper. While a child born on the first day is destined to be talented and to live long.

New Year: On New Year's Eve put out a shilling and a piece of bread and coal and bring them indoors on New Year's Day to ensure money, food and fuel throughout the coming year.

November: A hard frost before St Martin's Day (11 November) means that the ensuing winter will be wet, rather than cold:
> *Ice before Martinmas enough to bear a duck,*
> *The rest of the winter is sure to be but muck.*

Onion: An onion hung in a room will keep away disease. (There may be some truth in this, as a cut onion does attract germs). An onion placed under your pillow will make you dream of your future lover. A young girl who cannot choose between two lovers should cut the name of each man into the skin of two onions, then put the onions in a warm place. The first one to sprout will indicate the truer love.

Opal: Opal is rated unlucky jewellery.

Orange: The orange has long been regarded as a lucky fruit, and the orange blossom as a symbol of fertility, which is why it is

56

'Rooks building their nests high indicate that a
fine summer is coming.'

traditional to have orange blossom at a wedding. An orange
given as a gift by a boy to a girl, or vice versa, will encourage love
to grow between them.

Owl: If an owl is seen flying around your house or alighting on your
premises in daylight then disaster is forecast.

Pack of playing cards: Older generations of gypsies considered it
very unlucky to have a pack of cards in the *vardo* — caravan.

Pain: An old ritual is as follows:

If a child has a pain or has hurt themselves spit three times
whilst making a circle with the hand over the hurt, repeating:
Holy Kay, Holy Kye, that I come better gen ben bye,
*White sheep, black sheep, that'll come better by the end of the
week.*

Parsley: If you give it away, then you give away your luck, and if
you transplant it, your garden will be attacked by the Devil.

'Gypsies, in particular, regard the peacock as
the Evil Eye . . . '

There is a country saying that to sow parsley is to sow babies; and it used to be believed that eating quantities of parsley would put an end to an unwanted pregnancy.

Peacock Feather: Gypsies, in particular, regard the peacock as the Evil Eye and therefore would never bring a peacock feather indoors.

Pearls: Pearls mean tears for many people.

Pick up: To pick up dropped flowers in the road or anywhere out of doors will bring sickness.

Pillow: A pillow filled with hops will induce sleep.

Pin: *See a pin and pick it up, and all the day you'll have good luck.*
See a pin and let it lay, bad luck will follow you all day.

Potato: Carry a small potato in your pocket to ward off rheumatism.

Purse: Another Romany tradition is that when giving a purse as a present a coin inside will ensure good luck for the recipient.

58

'If an owl is seen flying around your house or alighting on your premises in daylight then disaster is forecast.'

Rabbits: On the first morning of the month, 'Rabbits!' should be the first word spoken, thereby ensuring a lucky month ahead. Miners in the nineteenth century hated a rabbit crossing their path on their way to work as this was considered very unlucky — indeed many would return home, fearing that disaster would take place in the mine.

Rainbow: To see both ends of the rainbow is considered a lucky sign.

Ravens: A raven croaking has usually been rated a bad omen. Yet at the Tower of London the raven is highly esteemed. In fact, an old belief is that if there are no ravens at the Tower, then disaster will overtake the country. Indeed the raven colony there, more than sixty years ago, became extinct: only one bird remained. An SOS went out, and one, William Palmer, a Dartmoor farmer and character, came to the rescue by catching some young ravens at Sourton Quarry and sending them to the Tower.

Miners, in contrast, saw ravens as birds of ill-omen. If they saw a raven flying overhead and its shadow passed over the mine shaft, they were usually reluctant to enter the mine until all the machinery had been thoroughly checked, believing the bird to be an omen for some forthcoming disaster.

Rust: If your keys or knives become rusty, it is an indication that somebody somewhere is building up a store of money which you will one day inherit.

Sailor: To touch the collar of a sailor was always considered lucky.

Salt: Salt has long been used in exorcism and fighting the dark powers of the Devil. In olden times when faced with an ordeal or difficulty, people would burn a pinch of salt 'for courage'. Times were when a bride carried some salt in her pocket during the wedding service 'for luck'. Spilling salt has always been considered *very* unlucky, but this can be counteracted by

'On the first morning of the month, "Rabbits" should be the first word spoken, thereby ensuring a lucky month ahead.'

throwing a pinch of salt over your left shoulder — the old people believed you were throwing it into the Devil's face. Even the much feared gypsy's curse can be rendered harmless by throwing some salt after the gypsy as he or she departs.

St Valentine's Day: A special day for all lovers, named after a young priest who was put to death for refusing to obey a law which prevented young men from marrying because it made them bad soldiers. The symbol of the day is the yellow crocus. A girl can foretell the type of man she will marry according to the bird she first sees on the morning of 14 February: e.g:

Blackbird	= priest
Robin	= sailor
Goldfinch	= a rich man
Sparrow	= a farmer
Bluebird	= a happy man
Crossbill	= an argumentative man
Dove	= a good man

If you see a woodpecker, then you'll never marry. It is, of course, very bad luck to sign a Valentine's card.

Saturday: Employees, coming to a new job on a Saturday, never stay long in that place of employment.

Scissors: A pair of scissors should always be 'sold' never given. Also never leave scissors lying open — bad luck.

Seagull: The sight of a seagull hovering above your house means news or correspondence from overseas.

Sea Superstitions: Superstition has run through generations of Westcountry fishermen — despite the strong influence of Methodism and John Wesley. Fishermen, for example, never mention 'long tails' or white rabbits before putting to sea. They also think it's bad luck to see a preacher on the quay — and few would consider launching a new ship or boat on a Friday. While down in St Ives, in the old days, local fishermen would never take saffron cake or a Cornish pasty with them on a trip.

Shivering: To shiver suddenly means that you have been touched by death, or that somebody has just walked over the plot where you will eventually be buried.

Shoes: Never put new shoes on the table — otherwise you will not prosper while you wear them. Always put your left shoe on first as this will bring you good luck that day.

Shooting Stars: If you see a shooting star, and make a wish before it

'A Seagull hovering above your house
means news or correspondence from overseas.'

vanishes, then your wish will be granted. Some people believe
that each star is a soul, and that shooting stars are on their way
to become the souls of new born babies. When someone dies, a
new star lights up in the sky.

Snow: When the snow doesn't melt, it's waiting for more to come.

Snowdrops: Old country folk would never permit snowdrops to be
brought into the home, believing they indicated sickness or
disappointment.

Soot: Soot falling down the chimney not only means you need a visit
from the chimney sweep, it is an omen that money is on its way.

Sorrow: If you pretend to cry, then genuine sorrow will soon follow
the pretence.

Spider: A Spider running down a small thread suspended in the room
denotes money coming unexpectedly. 'Never kill a spider if you
want to live and thrive' is an old Westcountry saying. In former
generations, if someone found a large spider inside the cottage or
house, they would pick it up carefully and put it outside the
building. (A beetle running across the floor was thought to be a
sign of rain.)

Spit: Spittle was considered to contain some psychic force. Hence the habit of the angler spitting three times on the bait, believing that this act would ensure a good catch. The market trader, too, often spat on the first coin of the day in the hope that it would bring a good day's trade. The act of spitting three times by the old country folk was rated a way of unwinding the bad luck of sighting a single magpie.

Spoon: Dropping a spoon forecasts a stranger coming to the door.

Sweeping Brush: 'Buy a sweeping brush in May, and you'll brush a member of the family away' is an old Westcountry saying, and many housewives, in the south-west, never brush sweepings out of the door for fear of sweeping their luck away.

Thirteen: A curious number because though it's traditionally regarded as an unlucky number, nobody has ever fully explained why. Christ together with his Twelve Apostles numbered thirteen. In the law courts those sitting in judgement number thirteen: a Judge and twelve jurors. Robert Graves, the poet, considers that all thirteens derive basically from the thirteen months of the moon calendars.

Toad: A toad entering the house denotes floods to come.

Trip: To trip going upstairs or on a step indicates a wedding, but 'dream of a wedding hear of a death'.

Walking: If you walk through a building without sitting down somewhere en route, you will never visit that place again.

Washing: If you wash in the same water as another person, a quarrel will develop. To avoid this unhappiness, make the sign of the cross over the water you share. 'Never wash blankets in May,' the old people said, 'or you'll wash a friend or a relation away.' And still on the subject of washing: a cat washing its face is a sign of good weather — 'Over the ear fair and clear.'

Water: Never throw water out of a window as it will be followed by tears.

Waves: Every ninth wave is supposed to be the biggest.

Whistling: Miners and fishermen have long considered it 'bad luck' to whistle on duty, and actors traditionally never like to hear whistling in the dressing room before a performance. 'A whistling woman and a crowing hen are the two unluckiest things under the sun.' It is also unlucky to whistle whilst rowing a boat — the old superstition being the boat will sink or get into trouble.

White heather: Brings good luck, and stops a drunkard from drinking. In Scotland, however, white heather is considered unlucky, as a bunch was given to Bonnie Prince Charlie when he landed in Scotland.

Wishbone: Supposed to be lucky, because of its horseshoe shape. If two people pull it till it snaps, then the person with the larger piece should wish, and the wish will be granted. In the North of England it is believed that if a young girl hangs a wishbone over her front door on New Year's Eve, the first man to cross the threshold will be her husband.

◄ Number 13: '. . . traditionally regarded as an unlucky number . . . '

'Travellers are a Superstitious Breed'

From Launceston I veered across Cornwall for my next interview. At St Anne's Chapel, roughly halfway between Callington and Gunnislake, I talked to Jeannette Broadway, wife of Acora, the Romany clairvoyant. They live in a modern bungalow, overlooking the Tamar Valley. From their windows you get almost a bird's eye view of miles of Cornwall and Devon, and you begin to understand how and why the River Tamar has helped to shape the personality of this corner of the Westcountry. A twisting grey ribbon of water, here and there sparkling in the sunlight, the Tamar virtually divides Devon and Cornwall and yet, in some mystical way, unites them.

'We, travellers, are a superstitious breed,' Jeannette openly admitted. 'We are brought up with superstition as children and it's something that never leaves you. It sticks in your mind as an adult, when common sense will sometimes say "That's nonsense!" But it's also a very personal thing. In a funny sort of way, people make their own superstitions too, and most people are superstitious, though they may not admit it.

'For example, we were at an airport recently and I found myself queuing up for check-point No. 13, and a friend, who was with us immediately left that queue because it was No. 13 and she went to No. 11 which had a far longer queue. And the interesting thing is that No. 13 remained the shortest queue all the time. People just refused to join it for fear of bad luck.

'Personally though I've had a lot of luck with No. 13 and have never found it unlucky in the slightest bit. I'm not afraid of Fridays either or even of Friday the 13th. In fact a lot of good things have

◄ Madame Jeannette: 'We, travellers, are a superstitious breed . . . it's something that never leaves you.'

happened to me on that date. As I say, you make your own superstitions or luck. . . up to a point anyway. I think there's an awful lot in that old Romany expression: "Think lucky and you'll be lucky!"

'Both my father and mother were travellers and therefore both were very superstitious. Fairground folk, like travellers, have it bred into them. I've been on a fairground, where they refused to use new machinery on a Friday, and lost a lot of money as a result. But nothing would make them alter their minds . . .this notion that you don't start something new on a Friday is ingrained in them.

'Never pass the salt . . . that's another old traveller's superstition. If you help a person to salt you help that person to sorrow. That's what they say. You'll never find my mother passing the salt to anybody.

'Travellers also believe that it's best for a man or woman to be buried where they were born. It's also unlucky to have a pack of cards in your trailer—that means caravan.'

Jeannette is a totally different interviewee from her husband. His words come out in a torrent. She weighs words carefully. With her hazel eyes, and wearing a headscarf, you don't have to ask if she has some Romany blood in her family tree.

'Like most women I am naturally interested in jewellery and, of course, Romanies have long considered that certain jewels are good luck bringers. Here then, according to age-old Romany lore, are the lucky gems for all signs of the Zodiac.

ARIES — Aquamarine and Bloodstone
TAURUS — Diamond
GEMINI — Emerald
CANCER — Pearl
LEO — Ruby
VIRGO — Peridot
LIBRA — Sapphire
SCORPIO — Opal (a word of warning here: this is very unlucky for all except Scorpio subjects!)
SAGITTARIUS — Topaz

Jeannette looking out of the 'vardoe'. 'If you _feel_ lucky, then the odds are you'll be lucky.' ▶

CAPRICORN — Turquoise and Zircon
AQUARIUS — Garnet
PISCES — Amethyst

'I believe that if you wear or carry something of your lucky jewel, when you've an important date or engagement, influences will usually be in your favour.'

Our conversation moved naturally to luck. Jeannette has a very positive policy here. She looked thoughtful as she sipped her coffee. If you *feel* lucky, then the odds are you'll be lucky. Luck, I believe, is largely a matter of feelings. It's hard to put into words, but I know when I'm *feeling* lucky. I might be at bingo or playing a game of cards, and I know, by this feeling, when I'm on a lucky winning streak. Likewise I often know when to stop . . . the feeling goes . . . another feeling comes over you . . . difficult to define but I recognise it.'

Jeannette's views stirred something in my memory. I recalled an old notion that if by some curious chance a hunchback crosses your path then you can expect either a further run of good luck — or a turning of the tide that will bring you better luck. Once upon a time the Monte Carlo casino employed a hunchbacked man for this very cunning superstitious purpose. Whenever a successful gambler was about to leave the table with his winnings, the management would instruct 'Mr Hunchback' to put in an appearance in the hope that the gambler might be tempted into trying his hand once more, believing that the 'winning streak' was still with him—while they hoped he might risk and lose all he had won.

From gambling our talk moved on to animals. On my way, I had seen a white horse and Jeannette agreed this was a good omen.

'Travellers have always seen animals as more than just animals. For example, if I see a white horse on a journey, say a white horse leaning over a gate as I'm driving along, I know, in my bones, that I'm going to have a lucky day. It's probably something to do with my upbringing in that my father loathed meeting sheep on the road. He'd pull his car into one side rather than split the flock. By

My father loathed meeting sheep on the road. He'd pull his car into one side . . . By splitting the flock, be believed he'd split his luck.' ▶

splitting the flock, he believed he'd split his luck.

'When you come to think about it, it's natural that animals should feature so prominently in superstitions because there are so many of them in the signs of the Zodiac, starting with Aries, the Ram, and going through to Pisces, the Two Fishes. As many as seven of the twelve signs are either animals or creatures of the sea. Seven and a half really, because Sagittarius is half horse and half man. So clearly animals are very wrapped up in our destinies.

'We've always associated a black cat with good luck too. Invariably if a black cat crosses my path, I put a wish on it. Another four-legged creature who is reputed to bring good fortune is the spotted Dalmatian dog.

'Now some people may think all this is a load of rubbish but Romanies have always treated such matters seriously, believing that some members of the animal kingdom are omens or luck bringers. I never kill spiders—would never think of it because of the ancient belief that they bring luck, especially in money matters.

'The other side of the coin is that I'd steer clear of houses with peacocks. Travellers have always rated the peacock as a bird of ill-omen capable of bringing illness, death, broken hearts and loss. Magpies too have a clairvoyant quality: one for sorrow and two for joy is the old saying. I wouldn't harm a robin but if I found one indoors or in the trailer, I should be very unhappy because we've always been taught that if a robin does appear in this way then it's an omen of death in the family, and many, many Romany folk will swear by this — the coincidences are too many.

'When we came to live near Callington, I immediately noticed a tree in the garden. "That's a lucky tree", I thought, and when my mother came she spotted it also. Gorgios (non-Romanies) would call it a mountain ash, but travellers refer to it as "the lucky tree". So if you find one in your garden, you'll know you're in the right place. But remember luck is largely a matter of feeling.'

Though, I've always been superstitious, ever since I can remember, I admitted to Jeannette that my superstitions had deepened since becoming her husband's publisher.

She smiled: 'Yes, I think the Romanies do spread superstition . . .

Magpies: 'One for sorrow and two for joy' is the old saying. ▶

72

**Dalmatian dog: '. . . reputed to bring good
fortune.'**

probably in the old days it was a means of generating business . . .
cashing in on the Gorgios wanting better luck.

'The Jews are superstitious too. A Jewish friend told me how
someone came into her house and said "How I envy you!" She made
this person spit and turn seven times. "It's unlucky if people envy
you," she claimed, and this little ritual unwinds the bad luck. The
Jews also believe that if you smash some crockery, something
valuable, this averts a break in a relationship, or the break-up of a
business or a breakdown in health. That's a comforting thought.'
Jeannette laughed. 'But you won't find me trying it deliberately!'

Old Nick in the South West

The Devil is reputed to have had some strong links with the West-country, but Cornish folk and Devonians have had some very different thoughts on the subject. Many Cornish natives insist that the Devil never crossed the Tamar—going West—for fear of being put into a Cornish pasty. While, in complete contrast, two old Cornish rhymes firmly put Satan in Cornwall.

> *Linkinhorne, where the Devil was born,*
> *Stoke, where the Devil first spoke,*
> *Gunnislake, where he made his mistake,*
> *Northill where he carries on still.*

That's how the first rhyme runs; and the second version spreads the Satanic net a little wider.

> *Directly after the fall,*
> *The Devil did enter Cornwall,*
> *At Hayle he first put on his tail,*
> *Then to Helston he went without fail.*
> *At Hell's Mouth he was seen as they say,*
> *Which place does remain to this day.*
> *At a town which is called Tuckingmill,*
> *It is said that he abideth there still,*
> *He refused to reside in Illogan*
> *Because they gave him a 'Floggan'.*

A third tale is that Satan did descend on a Cornish fishing village, and peeping through a cottage door saw a housewife in her kitchen making a conger eel pie. He enquired about the contents, and the lady summed him up perceptively: 'You must be the Devil they talk about,' she said, or words to that effect. 'Well, don't go interfering into matters that don't concern you . . . if you don't depart quickly, I'll put you into the pie. The story further runs that Satan departed immediately and landed at Devil Point, Stonehouse, just across the Tamar, hard by Plymouth Sound, where some say he still wanders restlessly.

On the other side of the Tamar, there are different Devon theories too. One is that he died of the cold in the Dartmoor village of Northlew. It's even been suggested that the monument erected, off the square, was put there to mark the event. Centuries back too gigantic footsteps were reputed to have been seen in the village. Another view is that Old Nick caught cold at the delightful stannary town of Chagford, and yet another is that he ate blackberries at the feast of St Michael at Barnstaple Fair, and being a glutton consumed too many—and subsequently succumbed.

Cornwall has more than her share of Saints and one theory why so many villages have perpetuated Saint names is as a means of guarding and protecting against Satan's possible return.

Whether he returned or not; whether he is dead or alive is a matter of speculation — and for the theologians. But the Devil is, at least attributed with one famous feat of architecture here in Cornwall. Indeed, it bears his name, The Devil's Hedge, though sometimes confusingly known as the Giant's Hedge. You'll find it near the lovely estuary village of Lerryn.

> *The Devil having nothing to do,*
> *Built a great wall from Lerryn to Looe.*

That's how an ancient Cornish rhyme goes, and he must have done a good job because many parts of the earthwork remain visible to this day between the coast and Lerryn. Historians tell us this was simply a sixth century fortification built by King Mark. But we, true Cornish, prefer to give the credit to old Nick. Yet I have to confess that I only got the Hedge's true location from a fellow Bossiney author, with Welsh blood. Sally Jones, in her *Legends of Cornwall* wrote:

'Surprisingly few people, even locals, knew of its existence when I investigated its whereabouts, and I drew a blank until the Lerryn farmer whose land it crosses gave me exact directions, including the great overhanging beech tree where a lane intersects it. Nowadays it is well camouflaged by a thick covering of bracken, bushes and trees, so I felt a real thrill of discovery when I "found" it for the first

76

time, a wooded bank, eight yards wide and fifteen feet high in places, striding proudly alongside Ribby Wood, vanishing and then reappearing again, the broad, broken swathe clearly visible from most hilltops between Lerryn and Looe.'

However the Devil was not always 100 per cent successful in this part of Cornwall. Back in the 1700s the area boasted a celebrated ghost-layer in the person of Parson Richard Dodge, Vicar of Talland. He apparently put the Devil to flight when he encountered him driving his black coach and headless horses. 'Dodge is come! I must be gone!' screamed Old Nick. A case of putting the fear of God into the Devil?

But there was by no means total acceptance of the story. Even some of Dodge's parishioners were convinced their Vicar was in league with the smugglers who infested that part of the South coast of Cornwall. Dodge's story of meeting the Devil was probably a

The Devil's Hedge: 'You'll find it near the lovely estuary village of Lerryn.'

cunning tactic to keep excisemen from a certain Bridle Path leading from Talland Beach.

In the eighteenth century Polperro was a favourite haunt of smugglers. Even today coming down the hill into the village, you get the gist of the geography and understand why the smugglers scored here: a creek cutting into a deep valley. Two hundred years ago it must have been a very secluded spot, not easily approached by land. That geography, combined with local co-operation, made it a splendid rendezvous for the smugglers and a constant headache for the authorities. One of the first Excise units was based at Polperro, but they got an unfriendly welcome from the local residents. Nobody would accommodate them, and they were forced to live aboard their boat in the harbour. The Cornish rated smuggling 'fair trade', and people from all sections of society took part. The gentry bought their brandy and lace at 'cut' prices, and Customs men often connived. The Cornish boatbuilders helped too in that they constructed swift-moving craft, clippers which 'could scud away from the fastest of the Government cruisers, and offer them a tow-rope in derision'. One Polperro vessel, the *Unity*, made as many as five hundred excursions.

◀'. . . a cunning tactic to keep excise men from a certain Bridle Path leading from Talland Beach.'

Meeting a 'Wise Woman'

My next interview took me back to one of my favourite corners of Bodmin Moor.

Commonmoor has the air of a private village, an impression intensified by a 'No Through Road' sign on the road above it. It lies in a sheltered valley below the Hurlers and Minions. Back in the 1800s this was mining country. Then engine houses from Caradon and Stowe's Hill, from Sharptor, Craddock Moor and Darley Tor were living things, belching smoke. Then more than a score of mines peopled the Moor hereabouts. But the noise of labour died long ago, and the ruined engine houses today stand like headstones in a cemetery.

Joan Bettinson was the reason for my journey. She lives in an old miner's cottage called Rose Vale in the village of Commonmoor, and has those blue eyes that I now look for in psychic people. Once upon a time she would have been called a 'wise woman' or 'white witch'. White magic was a form of magic employed *for good*. In ancient Egypt white magic is reputed to have divided water, exposing river beds and revealing long lost articles.

Joan Bettinson does nothing as dramatic as that, but she is one of a disappearing breed: she is a charmer. People come from all over Cornwall to see her in an effort to cure warts, and letters, from would-be patients, come tumbling through her letter box from all over Britain. She has also cured ringworm and has successfully treated shingles through the post—and by absent healing.

She is a perfect interviewee, in that she speaks slowly and chooses her words carefully. Within minutes of meeting we were on the same wavelength: not surprising really because we discovered we're as Cornish as Lanyon Quoit or Dozmary Pool, though there's some Breton blood in both our family trees. Joan Bettinson is a member of the old Cornish family, Marrack, who came from the Hundred of

Penwith down in West Cornwall. In *Cornish Mysteries* I wrote about her charming and the power and accuracy of premonitions, but, on this grey February afternoon, our second meeting, we concentrated on superstition and folklore.

'Like you I feel the origin of superstitions goes far back into the mist of time, a kind of religion, which is in many people today even though some will decline to admit it. May I suggest it is a kind of, shall I say, seventh sense, if there be such a thing, found more in the Cornish and Celtic natures. I have proved so many superstitions over the years:

'Throwing water out of a window has always been followed by tears, and, like Jeannette, I hate to see only one magpie and keep looking for a second—again I have proved that one correct on so many occasions.

'I believe too we Cornish can pick up the power from ancient

Joan Bettinson: 'Once upon a time she would have been called a "wise women".'

stones. I will tell you why I always touch the cross at Crylla. I have to pass through a field on my way back from Siblyback Lake where there is often a bull. This somehow gives me courage; also I feel a link with the past go up my arm—seems silly but true. I just put my finger up and across the incised cross automatically. Did you know that besides the Cheesewring or Wineglass stone, as it is sometimes called, there is a smaller pile of stones on the left-hand side? On the cap stone you will see what looks like a sort of carved seat scooped out by the elements and time. This is known as the Devil's Chair, and tradition has it that it is lucky to sit in it and make three wishes. There are also, if I remember correctly, three such scooped-out places caused by time and water; these are known as the Fairy Basins and are often filled with water. You are supposed to be beautiful forever if you splash the water on your face. These old folklore stories if not written down will be completely forgotten.'

Earlier that day I had visited the Hurlers, and even though much of the landscape was cloaked in a grey mist I still felt their magic. Contact with these aged, mysterious stones, for me, is not only a communion with the old people, but I feel a sense of peace and power seeping through. Many twentieth-century cynics would snort

The Hurlers: 'Contact with these aged mysterious stones . . . communion with the old people . . . '

derision, but you can talk about such things with Joan Bettinson easily and naturally. She has a wisdom and an understanding.

Some people have suffered a tingling sensation, rather like a mild electric shock, when touching segments of a stone circle. I cannot make such a claim, but I have felt physically, mentally and spiritually better for a visit to the Hurlers. There is, in fact, an ancient ritual relating to stones circles. Walk round them nine times, in a clockwise direction, the old folk said, and you'll get good luck and protect yourself from ill-wishing. As I say, you can discuss such things with Joan Bettinson. The circle, of course, has long been considered a source of power. A circular section of ground, prepared especially by a magician, was rated a 'safe place' against evil spirits. And the word 'circle' has come into our language in a significant sense: when people share a common interest they will often call themselves 'a circle'. Even the Zodiac is a circular plan; while time is usually measured by clocks, circular in shape, and many of our business transactions involve coins of the same shape. So the circle, regarded by many as the symbol of eternity, looms large not just in the Supernatural field but in Life as a whole.

Anyway, our conversation returned to superstitions. Here she can speak from personal experience—and she thinks the happenings are too frequent to be dismissed as 'sheer coincidence'.

She has some excellent methods of counteracting bad influences. 'For instance, it's bad luck to come back to a house, after you've started a journey, because maybe you've forgotten something. Well, *sit down* before going out again and that little ritual will unwind any bad influence. Now spilling salt . . . that's bad luck . . . here again there's another ritual: pinch up a little salt, between thumb and finger, circle it around your head three times and then throw it over your left shoulder. . .that way you'll have no trouble.'

I asked her about touching wood.

'If you want to stop something bad happening,' she explained, 'when the thought of that bad thing comes into your mind, make sure you *touch wood.* That act of touching wood will avert the bad. I believe "touching wood" stems from the Cross of our Lord. Not many parsons may like to admit it, but many of our superstitions stem from religion.

'Take that old belief that thirteen people around a meal table is unlucky—one will die before the year is out. That's an old super-stition, and almost certainly derives from the Last Supper.' She

'If you want to stop
something bad happening
. . . make sure you touch
wood.'

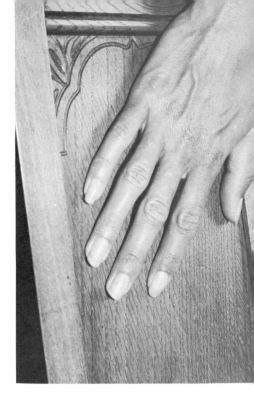

allowed herself a smile. 'I think not opening an umbrella indoors is another with religious origin . . . it all originates from the black umbrella being held over the clergyman's head at the graveside during a burial service when the weather's rough.'

Her most horrific experience concerned a family who came to stay with her at Commonmoor. One day, they decided to go down to Fowey.

'It was early evening, and I began to get worried because they had not returned,' she told me. 'A kind of premonition came over me and as I walked down the lane towards Rose Vale I was suddenly aware of an owl hovering over the roof of the cottage. Now it's an old tradition that an owl near premises in daylight is a bad sign, a very bad sign. Well, this owl alighted on the roof and I knew instinctively something terrible had happened to my visitors . . . and it was a bad omen.' Joan Bettinson went on to explain how they had gone out sailing off Fowey in treacherous water, against local advice, and had all nearly drowned. As it was the wife in the party had to be rushed to Truro Hospital.

'And there have been many, many cases where I have seen a traditional omen and it's been quickly followed by something bad. Not that superstition is all negative, all bad. There's a positive side to it . . . like seeing two magpies. I always feel better for the sight of that second magpie.'

On this, the positive side of folklore, Joan Bettinson firmly believes in the power of charms or talismans. 'I'm quite convinced that certain things do protect their owner or bring benefit and give good luck,' and just to underline her belief she disappeared into the kitchen and then returned with an old-fashioned wooden clothes peg. 'Take this for good luck,' she said with a smile. 'Sophie, a Romany out here on the Moor, made it. I always bought my clothes pegs from her, and whenever I go to Bingo I take one of Sophie's clothes pegs with me . . . it helps!'

Next day, wandering around a lovely peaceful churchyard in North Cornwall, I remembered Joan Bettinson's words. I thought too of the strange links between the Christian and Pagan religions —though basically miles apart, in some areas the dividing line is curiously blurred. It was only my imagination but in that quiet churchyard I thought I heard Joan Bettinson chuckle.

Fire and Folklore

Midsummer is one of the most momentous days in any folklore calendar. Personally I shall always have good reason to remember it because my whole interest in the subject of superstition, folklore and Supernatural possibility was triggered by a strange experience at Bossiney on Midsummer Eve in 1965: a shared experience I have described in *Supernatural in Cornwall,* an event that eventually grew into a book and ultimately helped to create a publishing business.

Here in Cornwall Midsummer Bonfires have been an old tradition. Moreover thanks to the energies of the Old Cornwall Societies, the tradition is still kept alive in certain parts of Cornwall.

The origin of the Fires goes back deep into Man's history. Originally a heathen festival, staged on hill tops, it was a form of Sun Worship. The Druids kindled their lofty fires on the first day of May month to celebrate 'the splendour of high summer'. The Fires, they believed, would bring blessing to the crop. But there was a gruesome side in that originally animals and sometimes criminals were sacrificed in the flames.

The early Church found itself in a dilemma. Suppress the pagan festivals or adopt and adapt them for Christian purposes? Wisely they chose the latter. So the fire ceremonies were allowed to continue with the Church's blessing—though they were now lit to celebrate the Eve of St John. Interestingly too some of the old pagan characteristics were retained, albeit in a disguised form. For example, instead of the gruesome living sacrifices, a symbolic wreath of herbs was thrown into the fire.

In the present-day ceremony, the Lady of the Flowers casts her bunch of herbs into the flames. There are 'good' and 'bad' herbs, the 'good' being plants of traditional medicinal power which are said to provide protection against the Evil Eye of Witchcraft; while the 'bad' herbs include weeds and plants that, over the years, are believed to 'possess malign influences'.

The colours of the ribbons which bind the plants are very significant too in that they are symbolic. The white ribbon represents strength; the green ribbon stands for knowledge and wisdom; blue for love; red sacrifice; and yellow the sun.

During the ceremony the Lady of the Flowers says these words:

> *In one bunch together bound,*
> *Flowers for burning here are found,*
> *Both good and ill.*
> *Thousand fold let good seed spring,*
> *Wicked weeds, fast withering,*
> *Let this fire kill!*

'In the present-day ceremony, the Lady of the Flowers casts her bunch of herbs into the flames.'

Robert Hunt, who studied our ancient Westcountry traditions so diligently earlier this century, devoted a chapter to Fire Worship in his *Popular Romances of the West of England,* first published in 1916.

'A few years ago,' he wrote, 'really but a few years—since, the stone altars on which the first inhabitants of these islands lit their holy fires had yet a place amongst us. In the village of Rosketall stood one such altar; in Treen was said to be found another. These huge masses of rocks, rendered sacred by the memories surrounding them, have been wantonly removed and employed in most cases in furnishing pillars at the "grand entrances" of the houses of squire farmers of the Land's End district; or they have been yet more rudely served, and are to be found at the entrance to a pigsty, or in the gate-posts to a potato field.

'The extinction of several of the old families is, to the present day, ascribed by the peasantry to the unholy act of removing or breaking up of the Garrick Zans in the village of Escols. The rock in the village of Mayon was called indifferently *table-mayon* (mōn), or the Garrick Zans. Within our memory is the gathering of the villagers around the Holy Rock. It was their custom, when anything was stolen, or a misdemeanour committed, to light a fire on this altar, and when the fagots were in full blaze, all those who sought to prove their innocence took a burning stick from the rock and spat on the blazing end. If they could extinguish the fire by spitting on the stick, they were declared innocent; but if the mouth was so dry as not to generate sufficient moisture to be heard "frizzing" on it, that unfortunate individual was suspected, if not declared, to be guilty. (Boys at school, to prove the falsehood of any charge, will take a stick from the fire and practise upon it in the same manner. May not the custom of joining hands and passing through the embers of a dying bonfire for good luck, be a vestige of the same ritual?) The Midsummer Bonfire was first lighted on the rocks in Escols, next on the Chapel Hill; then all other beacon hills were soon ablaze. Many superstitious rites were performed on the Garrick Zans, which are only found now as the amusement of young people on the eve of St Agnes and Midsummer.'

Some Cornish Folklore

Cornwall is rich in folklore. Not for nothing has it been called the Land of Legend. Yet I seriously doubt whether there can be such a thing as total myth, with no shred of reality.

Are we to dismiss all the giants as fairy stories? If so, how do we account for a coffin dug up in seventeenth-century Tregony measuring eleven feet and containing a tooth two and a half inches long? And what about the seven-foot skeleton found at St Michael's Mount? Doesn't that give substance to the belief giants once inhabited the Mount?

Anyway, I resolved to do a tour among just some of the folklore settings of Cornwall, and as a son of Penwith I began down in the claw of Cornwall, in the Hundred of Penwith.

Zennor Parish is one of the most beautiful in all Cornwall. Roughly five miles in length, stretching from Morvah in the west to Towednack in the east. North is the vast heaving of the Atlantic and facing it some of the finest cliff scenery in Britain: an awe-inspiring combination of granite and greenstone. This land and seascape have hardly changed since the days when Phoenician galleys sailed along this coast.

The Mermaid of Zennor is one of the most attractive, most romantic figures in the whole field of Cornish folklore. I'm biased in that I love Zennor and the legend, and I had the luck to see this church at Zennor, for the first time, decorated for Easter.

Mermaids appeared in Cornish legends before the arrival of Christianity to this most westerly land. Then they were symbols of Aphrodite, the Goddess of Love. Later, with the coming of the Cornish Mystery plays in the Middle Ages, the Mermaid's role changed to portray the two sides of Christ: half-God and half man just as she is half-woman and half-fish.

Once upon a time — as all good stories should begin — a beautiful

elegantly dressed woman attended services at this Church of St Senara at Zennor. Now though the Cornish have a bush telegraph system that could give MI5 a lesson or two, nobody knew her name or address. She was, in fact, a tantalizing mystery. But young Mathey Trewella, the squire's son, a handsome lad with one of the finest voices in the parish, resolved to solve the mystery. He, like half the male population, had probably fallen for her, so one Sunday evening he followed her down to the cliffs after the service. Neither were seen again. Years later a ship cast anchor in Pendour Cove and suddenly the Captain heard a beautiful voice hailing him from the waters below. It was a Mermaid with long strands of blond hair floating around her body who politely asked him to shift his anchor as it was blocking the entrance to her home under the sea and she wanted to get back to her husband Mathey and their children. A very frightened Captain returned to Zennor with the tale — seamen always associate Mermaids with bad luck — and after much discussion it was decided to put the Mermaid of Zennor in the Church as a warning to young men against the wiles of Mermaids.

And she is still there today, a carved figure on a bench end, mirror in one hand, comb in the other, long hair cascading over her shoulders. Local people have said that if you listen carefully on a moonlit night you can hear her singing, but I've never been that lucky. I have come on a night when the moon made an oily sea and Pendeen Lighthouse winked its regular patterns, but all I heard was the music of the waves.

At least I have Christine Quayle's lovely young voice on the *Sounds Like West Cornwall* record. Christine apparently came to live on the site of Mathey's old home, felt compelled to sing and became known professionally as the Mermaid of Zennor. The song recorded, *The Seagulls Scream,* she actually composed on the cliffs here at Zennor.

In Zennor churchyard one Cornish reputation is established, another dented. Dolly Pentreath of Mousehole, who jabbered away in the ancient Cornish language and begged for coins, claimed to be the *last* native speaker. She cursed those who declined to give her money, and was a memorable Mousehole character. But there is a

◀ The Mermaid of Zennor: '. . . if you listen carefully on a moonlit night you will hear her singing.'

stone standing in this Zennor churchyard which puts the Cornish language records straight. It reads 'to John Davey (1812 - 1891) of Boswednack in this parish . . . who was the last to possess any traditional considerable knowledge of the Cornish language. . .' As Dolly was in her grave before Davey was born there can be no argument.

Mousehole, however, is strongly rooted in Cornwall's folklore thanks to Tom Bawcock who is responsible for giving Penwith an extra Christmas celebration. Tom Bawcock's Eve falls on 23 December. A Mousehole man, Tom Bawcock lived roughly two centuries back. It had been a bad winter for fishing and there had been gales during which no fishing boats ventured out to sea. Christmas was fast approaching and still the fishermen of Mousehole were afraid to leave their harbour.

The eve of Christmas Eve came and still the gale was blowing, but Tom Bawcock got his crew together and said, 'Come on, me sons,

Den Tuthill: '. . . makes walking sticks with a difference.'

let's see if we can git our Christmas denner.' They set sail: the only boat. Local tradition has it that Bawcock and his crew had a good catch: seven sorts of fish in all they caught. The famous Starry Gazy Pie has these seven types of fish baked under a crust with their heads coming up through a hole in the middle of the pie and the song composed about it all runs:

> *A merry plaace you may believe*
> *Was Mouzel on Tom Bawcock's Eve*
> *To be there then who wu'dn wesh*
> *To sup o si bbm soorts of fesh.*

> *When morgy brath had cleared the path*
> *Comed lances for a fry*
> *And we had a bit of scad*
> *And Starry Gazy pie.*

> *Next come fairmaids*
> *Bra Thusty Jaades*
> *As maade our oozles dry*
> *An ling an haake*
> *Enough to make*
> *A raunin' shark to sigh.*

> *As aich we'd clunk*
> *As health were drunk*
> *In bumpers bremmen high*
> *an when up came Tom Bawcock's naame*
> *We praised 'un to the sky.*

★ ★ ★

Den Tuthill, a well-known Cornish landscape gardener from the Redruth area, is happily keeping a bit of Cornish folklore alive.

Den makes walking sticks with a difference. Each stick is unique — a shape and form of its own. He picks the woods from moorlands or woods or hedgerows all over Cornwall. 'Then I season the wood for six months,' he told me, 'strip off the bark and then polish, stain or varnish each one, and the result is a "Kellywyck".

But 'the difference' is deeper than the fact that each walking stick has a personality of its own.

'The whole business lies deep in legend,' Den explained. 'Details

93

'The bones of this land are not speechless.'

of the legend of the Kellywyck came into my possession some time back.

'Long ago, when Giants strode the moors and cliffs, Piskies wove their spells in the woods and glades of Cornwall, the Devil visited the land. Calling the Giants together he told them he now had some standing in the Underworld, and wanted something that would give him a certain dignity with the inhabitants of the nether regions. He would stay, he said, until it had been found. At this the Giants became very frightened — if they didn't do something quickly Cornwall would become a Hell on earth. They appealed to the Piskies, but although many potent spells were cast by them, wickedness spread across the land. Thunder rolled as the Giants went away grumbling, and huge boulders flew through the sky. Desperate, Jack, King of the Giants, went to see Joan-the-Wad, Queen of the Piskies, and meeting secretly in a cave at Holywell

94

Bay, they decided that Satan should be given a very special gift — something that would make the Old Devil go away for ever.

'In magic clothing, Jack went into the deepest forest, one which even Hobgoblins dared not enter, and there took from a certain tree a special walking stick. This was given to the Piskies who for seven days cast and wove their spells over it. When everything was ready, Giants, Piskies, and Hobgoblins from all over Cornwall met for the presentation on Bodmin Moor. Jack took the stick, and with Joan-the-Wad on his shoulder, strode to where the Devil sat on Brown Willy, breathing fire, Brimstone and wickedness. Now this was a very special stick — vicious spines protuded everywhere and flesh ripping thorns adorned the grotesque handle — nobody could touch it without protection, but the Devil knew he could and he was delighted. And when he took his walking stick, the spells woven by the Piskies were so powerful that the Devil felt compelled to walk — and he walked and walked right out of Cornwall for ever, leaving happy Giants to their rock throwing and gleeful Piskies to their spells.'

Now Den Tuthill says 'I make these walking sticks for this deliverance, but only the adventurous should use a Kellywyck because it puts the spring of youth into the user's step!'

★   ★   ★

From Den Tuthill and his walking sticks to the heights of Rough Tor on Bodmin Moor seemed a logical step. Whenever I come out on to the Moor I recall the painter Charles Simpson: the man who first made me see the Moor and begin to try and understand its magic. 'It is untamed land,' he told me, 'enduring sullenly the trappings of an age far from those remote twilights when with flint and stone man first sought to tame this wilderness.'

On high ground, such as this, I remember too another painter, Peter Lanyon, arguably our greatest native painter since Opie, who spoke of 'where giants may have hurled their googlies'. Painters can somehow get to the heart of the matter.

Out here on the Moor, you can get a strange sense of conflict. Pleasure — exhilaration at times — and yet unease. For all the antiquity and clarity of air — on the higher ground it is cold and pure — you can feel curiously vulnerable. A foot in the wrong place, the ground beginning to sag, the sound of oozing water and panic is not far away.

Not surprising then that Bodmin Moor has been the breeding grounds of so much myth and legend. Did King Arthur come this way? His hall remains a tantalizing Moorland mystery. Does Jan Tregeagle really haunt these parts? Does a ghost car travel these roads? The Moor poses many questions.

Interestingly, belief in the power of the stone circle is not dead either. Only recently a friend told me of a man who attempted to cultivate part of a common in 'spitting distance' of a well-known Westcountry circle. Within weeks of starting his project, he was taken seriously ill. Local folk shook their heads and said quietly 'The stones are getting at him . . .'

I was once told if we take the three-hundred mile journey from London to Land's End, we can travel also in time 'backwards to our beginning at an average rate of a million years for every mile of the journey'. It's a staggering thought and yet out here on Bodmin Moor, you begin to grasp all the implications and a sense of the past permeates whole chunks of the landscape.

Rough Tor is an awe-inspiring place. Long ago a building stood on this, the roof of Cornwall — some say two buildings were here — one, a chapel dedicated to St Michael. The construction of religious buildings on such lofty heights was because the old people saw the raging of a storm as something more than an angry facet of Nature. They interpreted the wind and the rain, thunder and lightning as a battle between the forces of the Devil and the Heavenly Host. They also had a comforting thought that sacred buildings, containing crosses and holy relics, keep the evil spirits airborne and away from the land below. Thus they reasoned, and so they built on high ground.

The rock formation here on Rough Tor is memorable. One cluster like coins stacked one upon another, by some miserly giant perhaps. Stones, weathered in such fantastic shapes, that you begin to realize Nature is a brilliant sculptor. Some, in the words of Daphne du Maurier, 'shaped like giant furniture, with monstrous chairs and twisted tables'.

The perceptive Frances Bellerby, of course, was absolutely correct: 'The bones of this land are not speechless.' There is something savage and primitive here. Moreover it has an elusive quality which you cannot easily pin to paper or paint on to canvas. Maybe it is best expressed in Nature's sculpture.

Some Dream Interpretations

As someone who dreams almost every night of my life, I have always been fascinated by dreams. I was therefore delighted to explore this subject further at a later meeting with Acora. 'We, Romanies, have long believed in the destiny of dreams,' he told me.

I am grateful therefore to him for help in compiling the following list of dream interpretations.

Dreams carry a message from our subconscious, often revealing fears and releasing hidden tension. There are literally hundreds of dreams and their interpretations — and sometimes a dream experience can contain more than one message. For instance dreaming of a beard needs very specific recollection. Was it a long beard? If so, the length of the beard indicates the dreamer will live to a ripe old age.

A black beard means something quite different: the blackness predicts trouble for the dreamer. While a dream of shaving off a beard forecasts disappointment.

In this short section I have deliberately concentrated on the positively good things we can expect in our dream lives.

Dreaming of an anchor signifies optimism and eventual success, an especially good dream experience for sailors.

An apron indicates 'kooshti duker', as the gypsies would say, meaning 'good fortune'.

Antiques: the arrival of an old friend or a forthcoming legacy.

A billiard table: a good sign for lovers, indicating lifelong loyalty.

A bath: provided the water is clear, an indication of good health.

A bride: happiness coming to the dreamer.

Chimney: if the chimney has smoke coming from it then there will be an inheritance.

A chicken: good news on the way.

A dog: faithful friendship.

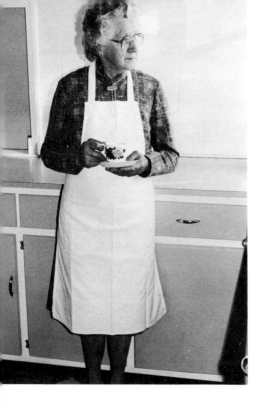 

**To dream of an apron indicates good fortune; of a
smoking chimney indicates an inheritance.**

A guitar: a romance going well.

Kitchen: a secret admirer is waiting on the wings of the dreamer's
love life.

A pyramid: a good omen — more than one pyramid suggests great
success for an ambitious dreamer.

A table: a very promising sign.

Zodiac: Acora stresses that to dream about *any* sign of the Zodiac
is usually a good sign and foretells that the dreamer will soon be on
strange soil.

These then are little more than a baker's dozen of hopeful dream
experiences. Acora however concludes: 'Some dreams are warnings
— rather like a gypsy's warning — and nightmares are always
ominous. In fact, a person who suffers recurring nightmares ought
to consult his or her doctor.'

Coincidences

Coincidences can be too numerous for the comfort of the cynic. I recall, for example, seeing a photograph of the former Conservative Prime Minister Edward Heath: a publicity shot in a bookshop helping to promote a novel by John Dyson entitled *The Prime Minister's Boat is Missing*. Five days later, on the second day in September 1974, Edward Heath's *Morning Cloud* III was lost. Curiously clairvoyant?

Author Colin Wilson, who lives at Gorran on the South Cornish coast, in the introduction to his best selling *The Occult* wrote of how once when he was searching 'for a piece of information, a book on one occasion actually fell off the shelf and fell open at the right page.' Colin Wilson returned to the theme of coincidence in his opening of *Strange Powers:* 'Reading a review of a recording of Verdi's early opera *Attila*, I saw a reference to a ballet called *The Lady and the Fool*, put together from early Verdi operas. I found his record on my shelves — I didn't know I had it — and discovered that the ballet had been arranged by John Cranko. The record notes mentioned that Cranko's other most popular ballet was *Pineapple Poll*, arranged from the music of Arthur Sullivan. I knew I had this, so I took it out, and played it after I had played *The Lady and the Fool*. At half past eight in the evening — immediately after playing the records — there was a programme I wanted to listen to on the radio; I switched on at 8-25. The radio happend to be tuned into the wrong station, and a news-reader was announcing the death of John Cranko, whose best-known ballets were *The Lady and the Fool* and *Pineapple Poll*. Not a tremendously exciting coincidence I agree but odd.

'I had probably possessed the record of *The Lady and the Fool* for years but never played it; I hadn't played *Pineapple Poll* for years either, and didn't know it was by Cranko. These were the only two records I played during that evening before the news of his death. 'Wells would say "Very well, what conclusion do you draw from that? That some invisible intelligence wanted to direct your attention to Cranko? Perhaps Cranko's ghost? Or that there was some mysterious working of providence . . . ?" No, I'm not suggesting either of these. I merely observe that coincidences of this sort happen sufficiently often to suggest that they shouldn't be ignored.'

Coincidences can indeed be curious.

In April 1982, we published *Strange Stories from Devon*, our 75th Bossiney title, and in it my co-author Rosemary Anne Lauder brought the book to a splendid thought-provoking climax with a chapter on the mysterious black dog of Devon. Various claims have been made about sudden inexplicable appearances, and vanishings, of this strange creature.

In the very week of publication, *The Tavistock Times* ran a factual report of yet another curious sighting by a Lydford farmer.

'An eerie black creature has been reported in Lydford. The creature is said to be about four or five feet long, built like a greyhound but with the back legs and face of a colt. Its eyes reflect no light.

'The creature was seen at about 3 am one morning by a farmer Mr Maurice Knowles on his land at Inglebrake, near Lydford. He spotted it as he went out to look after one of his ewes, which was about to lamb. It was snuffling its way alongside a hedge, looking, he thought, for a dead lamb. Mr Knowles had the creature in the light of his powerful lamp for ten minutes, and tracked it as it made its way beside the hedge. Before he frightened it off by shouting at it, he was able to look at its head, which resembled a colt's face.

"The funny thing was", he told the *Times*, "when I shone my torch in its face, its eyes didn't shine at all. I've heard that stags' and hinds' eyes don't shine back, but I haven't seen other animals like that." He thinks the animal may have been blind.

'The BBC say they were not filming *The Hound of the Baskervilles* that night, and the creature was too small to be the — probably mythical — Dartmoor puma. But there are many stories about giant and black dogs in Devon.'

The story in itself is interesting enough, adding further speculation to the numerous sightings of strange black cat-like animals in the county. The fact that this story was published during that week in April when we published a book whose cover was 'a ghost black dog' represents an extraordinary coincidence.

In talking to people who have seen ghosts, I have always been impressed by the matter-of-fact tone of many — the absence of ghosts in three-cornered hats or clanking chains. Many of the sightings, taken individually, could appear lightweight; taken collectively however they represent a solid body of evidence. And I find the same with coincidences.

Recently I paid another visit to Commonmoor to see Joan Bettinson. I had made no appointment; yet when Joan came to the door of the cottage she said: 'Oh, I was thinking about you last evening . . . and here you are this morning!'

Another strange coincidence came to me via Margaret Wainwright of The Cornish Arms, Pendoggett. Knowing my interest in such a subject, she kindly introduced me to Hilda Chapman who lives in a lovely old cottage alongside the inn.

Back in the early 1900s, her sister-in-law bought a small cottage organ for her daughter Annie. In due course, the daughter married and then died tragically in child birth. Perhaps naturally her mother decided to part with the organ, and it was given to a relation living in the town of Camelford.

Sitting in her cottage, 'Gran' Chapman, as she is known to all at Pendoggett, told me: 'One day, earlier this year, I went into the old family cottage down the road and there in the same room, standing against the same wall, was the same cottage organ. It was as if I'd gone back eighty years . . . I froze on the spot . . . it gave me such a turn!'

Briefly, it was an extraordinary chain of events. The relation in Camelford had decided to sell the organ, and put it in a sale at Tintagel, where the new owner of the cottage at Pendoggett — someone with no knowledge of the Chapman family—had bought it for his wife, an organ student, called Annie!

As Margaret Wainwright put it: 'The story of a cottage organ which insisted on coming home after eighty years.'

On the subject of this book, over our meal at the cottage, one evening, I confessed to Sonia 'I haven't a good idea for a cover for this one.' 'What about a black cat?' Sonia said, making it sound half like a question and half a suggestion. The next day, at our printers, Mike Frost in the art department, said 'Have you considered putting a black cat on the cover of this book?'

It sounded like an omen — too good a one to miss.

Acknowledgments

All writers are indebted to others. I am especially so on this occasion, for in addition to those people interviewed, others from both Devon and Cornwall have generously passed on thoughts and recollections. Above all, I am indebted to Michael and Hilary Wreford of Okehampton who have done such excellent research on the Devon side — two generous Devonians—and Jenny Slatter too who has given some valuable help on Devon matters. My thanks also go to Joy Francis, who has typed the greater part of the manuscript, my wife Sonia and secretary Janet Down, who have been about other Bossiney business while I have been digging into superstition and folklore, and last but certainly not least, Brenda Duxbury who has edited this, our 79th Bossiney title.

Books Consulted

Philippa Waring, *Dictionary of Omens and Superstitions,* Souvenir Publications.

Robert Hunt, *Popular Romances of the West of England,* Benjamin Blon

Peter Underwood, *Dictionary of Occult and Supernatural,* George G. Harrap

Alexander Howard, *Endless Cavalcade,* Z. E. A. Wade

ALSO AVAILABLE

STRANGE STORIES FROM DEVON

by Rosemary Anne Lauder and Michael Williams. 46 photographs.
Strange shapes and places — strange characters — the man they couldn't hang, and a Salcombe mystery, the Lynmouth disaster and a mysterious house are only some of the strange stories.
'A riveting read'.   The Plymouth Times
'. . . well-written and carefully edited'
                                        Monica Wyatt, Teignmouth Post & Gazette

STRANGE HAPPENINGS IN CORNWALL

by Michael Williams. 35 photographs. Strange shapes and strange characters; healing and life after death; reincarnation and Spiritualism; murders and mysteries are only some of the contents in this fascinating book.

'. . . this eerie Cornish collection.'   David Foot, Western Daily Press

CORNISH MYSTERIES

by Michael Williams. 40 photographs. Cornish Mysteries is a kind of jig-saw puzzle in words and pictures. The power of charming, mysterious shapes in the Cornish landscape, the baffling murder case of Mrs Hearn are just some fascinating ingredients.
'. . . superstitions, dreams, murder, Lyonesse, the legendary visit of the boy Jesus to Cornwall, and much else. Splendid, and sometimes eerie, chapters.'
                                                              The Methodist Recorder

SUPERNATURAL IN CORNWALL

by Michael Williams. 24 photographs. '. . . a book of fact, not fiction . . . covers not only apparitions and things that go bump in the night, but also witchcraft, clairvoyancy, spiritual healing, even wart charming . . .' Jenny Myerscough on BBC
'Serious students of ghost-hunting will find a fund of locations.'
                                                        Graham Danton on Westward TV

OCCULT IN THE WEST

by Michael Williams. Over 30 photographs. Michael Williams follows his successful Supernatural in Cornwall with further interviews and investigations into the Occult — this time incorporating Devon. Ghosts and clairvoyancy, dreams and psychic painting, healing and hypnosis are only some of the facets of a fascinating story.
' . . . provides the doubters with much food for thought.'
                                                        Jean Kenzie, Tavistock Gazette

OTHER BOSSINEY TITLES INCLUDE

GHOSTS OF DEVON
by Peter Underwood

DEVON MYSTERIES
by Judy Chard

LEGENDS OF CORNWALL
by Sally Jones

LEGENDS OF DEVON
by Sally Jones

KING ARTHUR COUNTRY
by Brenda Duxbury, Michael Williams, Colin Wilson

A CORNISH CAMERA
by George Ellis and Sarah Foot

DISCOVERING CORNWALL'S SOUTH COAST
by E.V. Thompson

THE CORNISH EDWARDIANS
by David Mudd

THE CRUEL CORNISH SEA
by David Mudd

CASTLES OF CORNWALL
by Mary & Hal Price

MY DEVON

MY CORNWALL

VIEWS OF OLD CORNWALL
by Sarah Foot

CORNISH CHURCHES
by Joan Rendell

MY DARTMOOR
by Clive Gunnell